Design with MongoDB

Best models for applications

ALESSANDRO FIORI

Cover design by: Stefano Bertotti

Translation by: Alberto Grand

Codice ISBN: 9798557417884

Casa editrice: Independently published

DEDICATION

To Sophie

DESIGN WITH MONGODB

CONTENTS

ACKNOWLEDGMENTS

This book is the result of years of work and study. However, its realization would not have been possible without the help and support of some special people.

A special thanks goes to Silvia. The long discussions have helped me to understand how best to realize my initial idea for this book. Her suggestions have been very useful to improve both the content and the structure of the book.

Thanks to Stefano for the realization of the cover. His ideas and graphic skills always give an original touch to every work.

Thanks to Alberto for his precious translation and revision of the english version of this book.

The biggest thanks go to my family. To Maria who supports and endures me in my every endeavour. Thank you for being my official reviewer. To Francesco for making me play and go out. Sometimes it is the best way to find ideas. To my parents who supported me during my studies. And finally to Sophie, my canine companion of a thousand adventures.

A final thanks goes to the readers and to those who would like to send me their suggestions. I hope that this book will be useful for your professional career.

FOREWORD

Nowadays the management, storage and analysis of big data, i.e. large collections of heterogeneous data, plays a fundamental role in many application contexts. The transformation of raw data into knowledge, somehow present but "hidden" in data collections, is potentially of great importance for organizing and planning activities in a "company", in all of its various form.

Until the end of the last century, relational databases were unquestionably the reference technology for data management. However, the increasing amount and heterogeneity of data, favoured by a greater diffusion of the internet and all of its applications, such as social networks, have uncovered some major limitations of the relational approach.

NoSQL databases are today's de-facto alternative to relational databases for managing large collections of heterogeneous data. NoSQL databases are schema-less databases, i.e. they do not require the definition of a fixed data schema. This feature introduces a significant degree of flexibility in data modeling, as the data representation may easily adapt to any new requirements that must be managed by applications. However, if on the one hand the schemaless approach offers greater flexibility in representing data and has the potential to speed up application development, on the other hand it introduces new critical challenges regarding the optimal management of heterogeneous information and the quality of stored data.

This book presents some of the patterns most commonly used in various application contexts for modeling data in a NoSQL database.

MongoDB, one of the document NoSQL databases having gathered the most popularity in recent years, was chosen as a reference case in the textbook. Since its latest versions, MongoDB has started to include features (such as the pipeline aggregation function and transaction management) that make it a suitable choice for a variety of contexts, thanks to its improved reliability and the capability to perform complex queries efficiently.

In this textbook, patterns for data modeling are introduced through discussion of case studies. This approach aims to point out the possible advantages and disadvantages of a modeling solution chosen to meet the needs of specific contexts. Finally, the last section includes useful questions as an additional learning tool for verifying the concepts presented.

The book is therefore a useful support to approach the design of a NoSQL database.

Silvia Anna Chiusano
Associate Professor
Polytechnic of Turin

INTRODUCTION

In the digital era, data has become the beating heart of the economy. The analysis of the immense amount of data produced by new technologies has been by far the most trending topic in recent years. Suffice it to say that the "data scientist" is now one of the professional figures most sought-after by companies and one of the most coveted professional careers. Unfortunately, in this race for data analysis, we ended up losing control of it. What do we mean? The answer is simple and unsettling at the same time: how do we organize and save data?

Many business and not-for-profit organizations, especially the small and medium-sized ones, are still relying on outdated or unstructured data storage systems. Relational databases, the technology that dominated the years at the turn of the century, were relegated by professionals to mere data storage tools. This also meant that relational modeling, i.e. the design of data structures in relational databases, has become a topic of little interest, if not altogether left to chance.

Unsurprisingly, some organizations are using spreadsheets to save their data in a semi-structured way. In a few, less unfortunate cases a relational database (e.g. Access) is indeed used, though it often consists of only one large table. You may hardly believe this but, unfortunately, reality and the theory presented in university courses are still a long way apart from one another.

Designing a database well is a fundamental prerequisite to optimizing any task ahead, even with advanced tools. Data scientists will be happy if they can deal with "clean" and structured data, as this partly simplifies their work and allows them to obtain greater reliability with their analyses. This book will show you how to structure a *document-oriented NoSQL database,* based on MongoDB technology.

Designing a database

Database design is one of the most discussed topics in computer engineering books and courses. For relational databases, several models and patterns have been studied, presented, and are used daily by designers. In fact, the relational model helps to define more stringent rules on how to represent the data one wishes to keep track of.

NoSQL databases, which are by their very definition *schemaless*, i.e. without schema, suffer from the lack of a specific formalism and clear and well-defined rules. Therefore, designing this kind of databases becomes more of an art than a mere engineering exercise.

The question that all users of NoSQL databases, and in particular those of MongoDB, ask when they first start using them is the following: How do I structure the data schema? The answer, as in many engineering fields, is: it depends. Unfortunately, there is no single solution to the problem, but you need to study the context, some of the sample data in your possession, and the use cases related to the applications that will rely on our database.

So, you need to ask the right questions to get the right answers. For example: How many read and write operations will the applications do? What data will be displayed together? What types of performance do we need? How large are our documents/entities? Are the number and the structure of fields within each document stable, or will they change over time? Can we predict how the data will grow?

The answers to all these questions, and many others, will influence how the database will be designed. Although the database is schemaless, the basic schema that we will define based on the applications is fundamental to achieving the best performance. In fact, many problems related to disappointing performance are due to poor modeling.

As you will see in more detail in the next chapter, many NoSQL databases use a document-based data model. This type of model is highly flexible and can track any type and structure of data that your applications will handle.

Flexibility is both the blessing and the curse of these databases. In fact, it can represent any type of data, but at the same time it may lead to much more complex schemas than are actually needed. Therefore, when designing, you should keep performance, scalability, but above all simplicity in mind.

Book structure

The book is structured in three sections.

The "Prerequisites" section introduces the basic concepts of NoSQL databases and, in particular, some features of MongoDB, which will be used as a reference database for the rest of the text.

The "Case Studies" section analyzes some application scenarios with the purpose of defining models that exploit the potential of document databases and in particular *MongoDB*.

Finally, the "Learning checks" section presents some exercises to verify the skills acquired through the case studies and to show how the models analyzed can be reused in similar contexts.

But why MongoDB? The choice to deal only with MongoDB is due to the fact that nowadays it is the most widely adopted NoSQL database, as well as the one offering an excellent compromise between NoSQL flexibility and relational performance, as we will discuss in Chapter 1 "A short overview of MongoDB". We will see, in fact, that this database provides both the flexibility and the performance typical of NoSQL databases, with some extra features of relational databases such as transactions.

The case studies presented in the book are:
- e-commerce website
- Internet of Things (IoT)-based monitoring system
- Information system for a medical center

These scenarios have been selected because they are current contexts, but above all because they present very interesting data modeling problems. They will range from managing the heterogeneous characteristics of the items sold by an online store to correctly saving time series of sensor data, to evolving a database without necessarily compromising application behaviour.

The issues that we will address will introduce modeling patterns useful to optimize the performance of our database. The patterns [1] that we will analyze will be the core building blocks for a more methodological style of database design. They can also be partially reused them with other types of

NoSQL databases, by adapting them to the characteristics of the chosen technology.

Figure 1 shows a diagram that illustrates which modeling patterns are used in each case study.

Case studies

Modeling patterns	E-commerce website	Internet of Things	Medical center
Tree	✓		
Approximation		✓	
Attributes	✓		
Buckets		✓	
Document versioning			✓
Extended reference	✓		
Outliers	✓		
Polymorphic	✓		
Pre-aggregates		✓	
Prealloacation			✓
Schema versioning			✓
Subsets	✓		

Figure 1 Usage of models within the case studies.

We hope, therefore, that these modeling exercises will give you food for thought and useful tools for a more conscious and less "artistic" design of your databases. Art is creativity, but it also needs methods to express itself at its best.

Who is this book for?

This book is not intended as a guide to discovering MongoDB and all of its features. Therefore, you should not expect to find instructions on how to install and configure MongoDB on your PC or server. As a matter of fact, we are not even going to study in detail how to query and manipulate data in the database, or how to create a pipeline aggregation for analyzing it.

Instead, what you will find is a collection of case studies that will allow you to understand how to use the features of the document database par excellence (MongoDB) in order to optimize the structure of your database.

To provide you with a starting basis, the next chapter will introduce the fundamental concepts and main features of MongoDB. For more information about the functionality of this database, you can always refer to the official documentation [2].

Beyond the book

Additional material is available free of charge on the web page dedicated to this textbook: https://flowygo.com/en/projects/design-with-mongodb/. You can contact the author through the website and find other useful information to start off in the world of databases. Visit https://flowygo.com/ to stay updated.

SECTION I
PREREQUISITES

CHAPTER 1
A SHORT OVERVIEW OF MONGODB

Before diving into the main features of MongoDB, some basic knowledge of NoSQL databases is in order. This type of databases has seen its rise in the last decade, but its history begins at the end of the last century. In particular, the term "NoSQL" was used in 1998 by Carlo Strozzi at a meeting in San Francisco where he presented his database. This database was primarily intended for developers, who could query it via shell scripts instead of the SQL standard language.

The idea of using different models to save and query data began to take hold and for years new technologies were developed that revolved around this concept. Under the NoSQL database shell, a variety of different technologies exist, each with its own assortment of open source and commercial products. Databases are mainly divided into the below categories:

Key-value: they are based solely on key-value pairs. They do not normally use complex structures, but they are highly efficient.

Column: data are saved in columns. Each column represents a (possibly complex) attribute. Rows are reconstructed by combining several columns.

Graphs: based on graph theory, they represent entities as vertices in a graph, while relations are modeled as edges. They are powerful tools for representing contexts with a high degree of mutual interaction among entities, such as social networks.

Document: they are based on the key-value paradigm but can contain complex structures. Each document represents an instance of an entity with all of its properties. They can easily capture the various facets of different instances and save complex hierarchies among the data.

Regardless of their specific implementation, all of these databases share the following set of features:

Schemaless. They do not require a predefined model for the database and its data structures, as in relational databases. This feature offers the freedom to save heterogeneous information without necessarily defining a schema *a priori*.

Non-relational. In relational databases, connections between data are established using external keys, i.e. references to records from other tables. In NoSQL databases this connection is expressed with other structures. For example, document databases commonly embed information in the referencing document, while edges are used to represent interconnections between data (vertices) in graph databases.

Scalability. NoSQL databases were born with the aim of providing more scalability, both horizontally and vertically, in mind. The most popular database architectures exploit server clusters to efficiently manage queries and data manipulations.

Each database provides specific functionality, based also on its category. Finding the best fit for an application scenario of interest is always a complex process that does not admit a single correct solution. Like in many branches of engineering, the answer to the question "Which database is the best solution for my application?" is: it depends.

The factors that influence the choice range from the required functionality, depending on the use context, to each developer's specific knowledge of technologies. For these reasons, it is difficult to provide guidance on how to choose the best database for our needs.

Instead, we will focus on how to get the best performance from a document database, specifically MongoDB, through the choice of suitable data models.

1.1 MongoDB: a history

The document database that, according to many experts, corresponds to the best compromise between NoSQL and relational database features is MongoDB.

MongoDB, or more simply Mongo, was first released in February 2009, after two years of development. Since then, several versions have been released. At the time of writing this book, the latest available version is 4.4, officially released on July 30, 2020.

Over time, Mongo's capabilities and functionality have evolved to become one of the most popular NoSQL databases. But what is the secret of its success? It's hard to say, but the possibility to create very complex as well as flexible data models has played a key role, allowing the database to adapt to almost all situations we may put it to the test.

Furthermore, in recent years, with the introduction of the **aggregation pipeline** and **transactions**, the quantum leap has been significant. Using the pipeline aggregation, we can create queries that combine and transform our data in order to extrapolate real-time analysis. The introduction of transactions, the lack of which has been NoSQL's Achilles' heel since its inception, enabled Mongo to attain much the same level of functionality and reliability provided by relational databases. Currently, it is possible to take the database from one consistent state to another even when multiple documents are involved in a transaction. The documents written within a transaction are then consolidated into the database if, and only if, no errors have occurred in the meantime. Otherwise, a rollback is performed. This aspect, which was always the workhorse of relational databases because it could ensure great reliability, can no longer hold the data architect back from shifting to NoSQL. To learn more about these issues please refer to the official MongoDB documentation [2].

To better understand the usefulness of NoSQL, we will focus on database modeling. Although NoSQL is schemaless, i.e. without a default schema, a structure must be defined for our documents (or, else, managing our data would be impossible). In the following chapters we will analyze some case studies and identify good practices for data modeling. However, before we delve deeper into our study, we need to introduce some basic concepts that will be reused throughout.

1.2 Data structure

Let us start from the structure used by Mongo (as well as all NoSQL databases of the same category) for representing data: the document. This is a database record whose structure is made of multiple key-value pairs, similar to JSON objects. The key values, also called **fields**, can include complex structures such as arrays or documents. In the latter case we speak of **embedded document**. In Figure 1.1 an example of a document describing a user is shown. It includes both "simple" fields, i.e. composed of simple key-value pairs, and nested documents.

```
                              User

  {
  "_id": ObjectId("31cf91add3454f14688944db"),
  "name": "Alessandro",
  "sex": "M",
  "groups": ["Python", "Lego"],
  "birth_date": ISODate( "1982-12-14"),
  "contacts": {
              "tel": "+390123456",         ⎤
              "email": "info@flowygo.com"  ⎬  Embedded document
              },                           ⎦
  "publications":[
              {"title": "Design with MongoDB",
              "year": "2020"},
              {"title": "Document Summarization",
              "year": "2019"}
  ], ...
  }
```

Figure 1.1 Structure of a document.

Embedded documents are mainly used to capture the relationships between data without having to split the information into separate documents. This model is called **denormalized**. Its use aims to speed up the retrieval of a document's related information without resorting to JOINs like in relational databases. Unfortunately, in some cases, this solution involves the duplication of data and the implementation of appropriate strategies to manage the consistency of the duplicate information.

It is also possible to insert a reference to other documents in a document by **reference**. These represent the value of the identifier, i.e. the _id field, of another document. Similar to the concept of table in relational databases, documents are organized in **collections**. It is therefore possible to create references between records belonging to the same collection, or to different collections.

Building on the example in Figure 1.2, it is possible to create two collections to save information about a user's contact information and publications, respectively. Within the documents of these two collections, a *user* field will be inserted holding the identifier of the document belonging to the *User* collection.

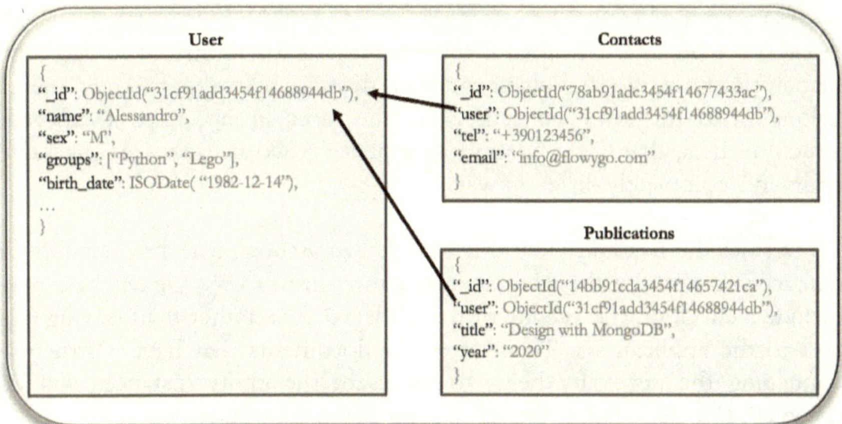

Figure 1.2 Example of using references to create relationships between documents.

This approach, which derives from relational database modeling, could negatively affect the performance of our application. In fact, every time the application needs the contact information and/or publications of a user, it will necessarily have to query the other collections, increasing the number of database accesses accordingly.

Therefore, be careful not to abuse it. Mongo does not provide a native JOIN operator! Therefore, it is not possible to combine information from two documents within a single query. The only possibility is to use the pipeline aggregation with the *$lookup* or *$graphLookup* functions.

These two functions can merge data that are linked together into a single document. The *$lookup* command performs a left outer join between a document and documents containing the value of a certain field. The documents in the collection that meet the join condition will be added to an array within the source document. On the other hand, *$graphLookup* performs a recursive search in a collection to find all documents that are linked together, starting from an initial document. This function is very useful if the documents in the collection represent a tree or a graph.

In terms of execution time, these solutions provide much worse performance than accessing a single document. In fact, the pipeline aggregation requires more databases accesses and, in some cases, it may not terminate correctly, due to excessive resource demand. For these reasons, embedded documents are one of the most used and recommended choices in some scenarios.

As mentioned earlier, the great advantage of all NoSQL databases is the "lack" of a schema. In Mongo, this feature has an additional implication, namely **polymorphism**. Polymorphism is the possibility that two documents belonging to the same collection, i.e. the same group, have a different structure. It is, therefore, possible to represent two instances of the same entity in a completely different way.

Despite the flexibility that our models can assume, it is also possible to enforce validation of the document structure. In this way, the database may include a check on the validity of the managed data, rather than leaving this task to the applications. Therefore, only documents that have a structure containing the necessary fields to represent the entity instances will be accepted. For these fields, the value must also belong to the correct type.

It should also be remembered that the atomicity of the operations is always guaranteed at the document level. Therefore, a write operation (i.e., insertion, update or deletion) will be consolidated on the database if an error or failure does not occur at the same time. In order to guarantee the atomicity of operations spanning multiple documents it is necessary to use transactions, which are available only in configurations exploiting replica sets. Otherwise, it is advisable to use models based on embedded documents. We will later see how to apply these models in an appropriate way.

To get good performance out of our queries, it might be necessary to create **indexes**. These are secondary structures that store some information from our documents, in order to optimize their search. If defined properly, idexes can significantly speed up the most frequent queries. On the other hand, the database will use more disk and memory space to save and use them. In addition, writing operations may be slowed down – especially if too many indexes were defined. Among the most interesting indexes available in Mongo is the Time To Live (TTL). This index determines survival time for a document within our database. Once this time has expired, the database itself will delete it through an internal routine. We will see later when this index can be used in combination with templates.

We now possess all of the information needed to better understand the case studies that we are going to analyze and, above all, the models that we will define and use. Let the fun commence!

1.3 Learning checks

In the following, you will find some questions to help you evaluate the knowledge you acquired in this chapter. Complete answers can be found in Section III "Learning checks", in the chapters indicated under the "Answer" column.

Question	Answer
What does polymorphism allow?	Chapter 5.1
How and when can atomicity be guaranteed on multiple documents in Mongo?	Chapter 5.2
What are the main features of NoSQL databases?	Chapter 5.3
Which Mongo function can be used to analyze data saved in a collection, or integrate information from different collections?	Chapter 5.4
What types of NoSQL databases can be used to model a social network?	Chapter 5.5

SECTION II
CASE STUDIES

CHAPTER 2
DESIGNING AN E-COMMERCE WEBSITE

E-commerce websites have increased exponentially in recent years. Even small businesses are gradually converting to digital, bringing their commerce to the internet. Many e-commerce sites use well-established technologies such as Woocommerce [3], Magento [4], Shopify [5]. Let us try to imagine building a new e-commerce website with some features similar to those of Amazon, based entirely on Mongo.

The e-commerce site will have to manage different products belonging to different product categories. Each product will have its own characteristics. Some of these will be common to all, while others will be peculiar to single products. Different characteristics may also be found among products belonging to the same merchandise category.

The products are divided into categories, which are organized in a hierarchical way. Each category can contain different products, while a product belongs to only one category. The hierarchy of the categories of each product needs to be managed in an appropriate way, both for storage and for display.

Within the database, customers and product orders will have to be managed. An order is made by a customer and can contain several products. For each purchased product, it is necessary to keep track of the quantity ordered and the price applied at the time of order processing.

We also wish to store customer reviews, both as a way to offer a feedback facility for the products in the catalog, and to help new customers find the best product for their needs.

In the next sections, we will analyze the requirements for the e-commerce site, identifying the models that can improve the performance of the database.

2.1 Polymorphic model

Let's start from the heart of the new e-commerce: the products. We will assume that the products offered are very different from each other and span categories such as cameras, smartphones, books, and movies. Each of these should have specific features that will help the customer to choose the best product for her needs. However, some of them are common, such as *brand*, *product name*, and the *description* field. We need to find a solution to manage in a homogeneous way something that is actually very heterogeneous.

A first possibility is to create different collections for each product category. For example, we could create a collection for cameras and one for books. In principle, these collections could allow us to treat the characteristics of the products in a different and specific way, depending on the product category. Figure 2.1 shows an example of a document for each of the two collections.

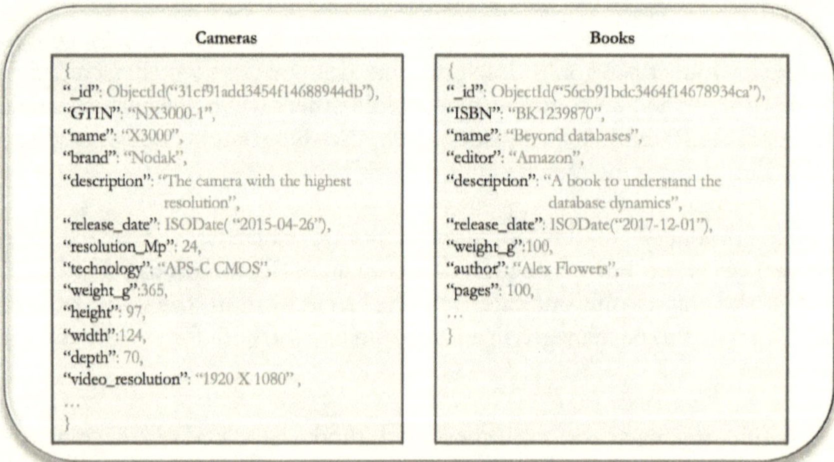

Figure 2.1 Example of collections for e-commerce products. Each collection contains only the products of a specific product category.

But what if we wanted our site to display on a single page the list of characteristics of products belonging to different categories? Or simply show information about products that were recently viewed by the user? We would need to access different collections and build the pages in a very articulate way, in order to adapt to the document structure of each collection.

Furthermore, can we actually guarantee that all the products within each category we have defined will always have the same characteristics? In many cases, unfortunately, we can't. Just think of electronic products in general. Two smartphone models differ in many cases for at least a couple of features. For example, models from a few years ago had only one rear camera, while newer models have even 3 or 4 cameras. Therefore, if we wanted to store the resolutions of each rear camera as a separate feature, we would have to create further subcategories and, sticking to the model used (i.e., one collection per product category), we would also have to create new collections. This solution is difficult to manage from various points of view.

We need an alternative that allows us to save all our products in a single collection, but also helps to dynamically list the characteristics of each product. We can define a document as shown in Figure 2.2.

Products

```
{
  "_id": ObjectId("31cf91add3454f14688944db"),
  "code": "NX3000-1",
  "name": "X3000",
  "brand": "Nodak",
  "description": "The camera with the highest
                  resolution",
  "release_date": ISODate("2015-04-26"),
  "weight_g":365
},
{
  "_id": ObjectId("56cb91bdc3464f14678934ca")
  "code": "BK1239870"
  "name": "Beyond databases",
  "brand": "Amazon",
  "description": "A book to understand the
                  database dynamics",
  "release_date": ISODate("2017-12-01"),
  "weight_g":100
}
```

Figure 2.2 Example of two documents related to different products (a book and a camera) containing only the common fields.

The structure of the document will contain some fields that are common to all products, such as *name* and *brand*. These fields are usually the ones we identify as fundamental to describing the objects within the application. To help us, we can also make use of ontologies, such as Schema.org [6], which provide an overview of how objects, people, events can be described in a formal and structured way. Returning to our problem, however, we still need to understand how to include the characteristics of the products in each document in the collection.

A possible solution is to insert the characteristics as additional fields of each document, as shown in Figure 2.3.

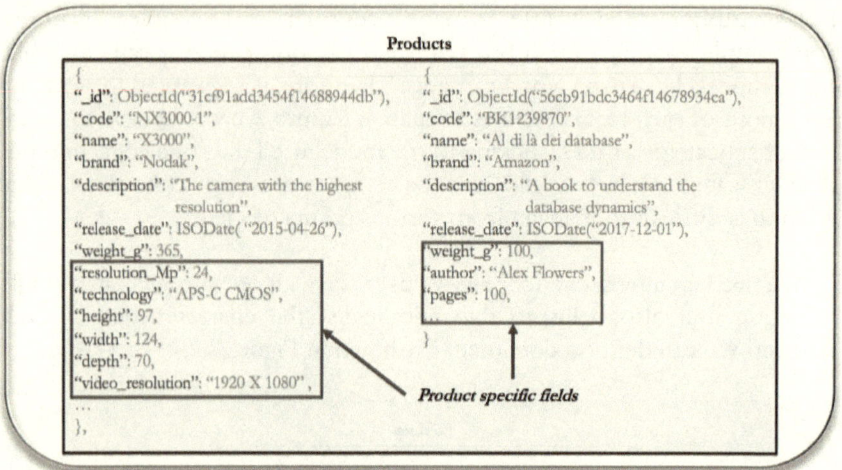

Figure 2.3 Collection of products using the polymorphic model.

In this way we can keep track of any feature without having to resort to different collections. This model is called **polymorphic** and allows us to accommodate documents with some differences within the same collection, helping to improve the performance of our queries. In fact, in order to access the information of each product we do not have to differentiate our queries based on groups defined beforehand, such as the product category. We can also incorporate different products in the same page of the e-commerce, without complicating the logic for querying and displaying product sheets.

From a practical point of view, in the context of our case study, this solution involves some limitations. For example, to visualize a certain characteristic we must first verify that it exists, and then manually manage its "meta information", such as the label, the category, etc.

We can also apply the polymorphic model to embedded documents. Thus, our catalog can be modified by creating an array of embedded documents that will contain all the specifications of a product. The subdocuments contained in this vector will also have a similar structure, which may vary according to the product specification. The structure will be, for example, the one shown in Figure 2.4.

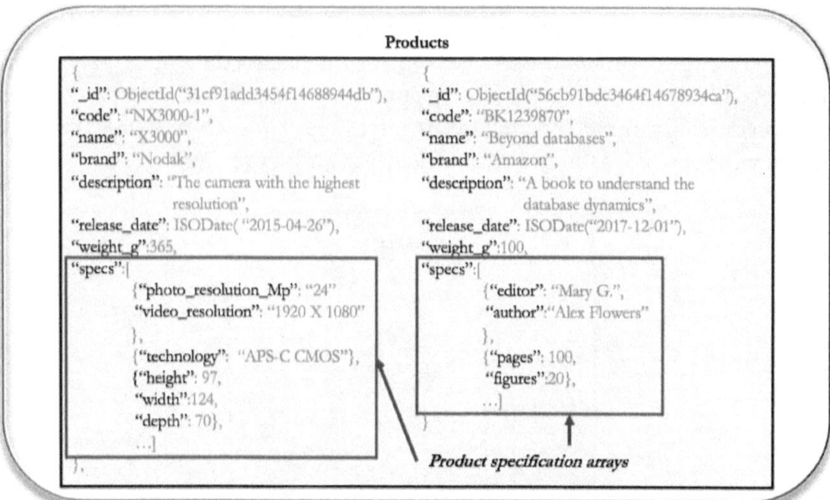

Figure 2.4 Application of the polymorphic model to the specs vector containing the specific characteristics of each product.

2.1.1 Pros and cons of the polymorphic model

The polymorphic model makes it possible to store, within the same collection, documents that only differ on some of their characteristics. It is usually applied when accessing the entities to be modeled regardless of their type is required; there are also typically more similarities than differences among the documents. However, it mandates that the application properly manage the differences between the various documents, for both database reads and writes.

The advantages and disadvantages of using this model are summarized in Figure 2.5.

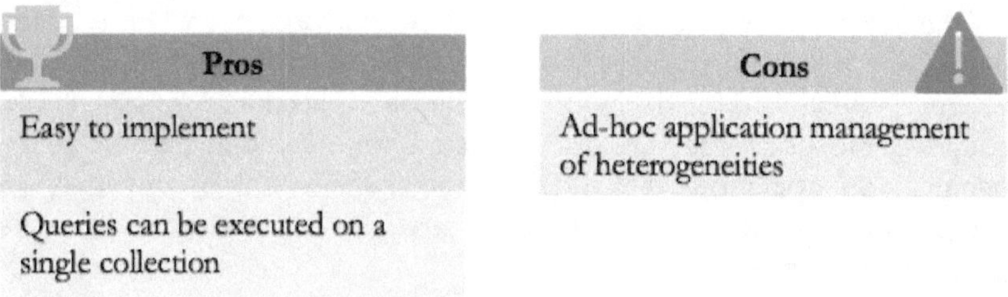

Figure 2.5 Pros and cons of the polymorphic model.

2.2 Attribute model

Sometimes we may need to query or sort our products by a set of fields that share a common feature. An example is the release date of a movie. Each movie has release dates that differ by country. A possible solution is to apply the polymorphic model by creating specific fields for each country where the movie was released, as in the example shown in Figure 2.6.

```
                         Products

{
"_id": ObjectId("42ae92bdd3454f17698946ea"),
"code": "F100021",
"name": "Avengers: Endgame",
"brand": "Marvel",
"description": "La battaglia finale contro Thanos",
"release_date_IT": ISODate( "2019-04-24"),
"release_date_MX": ISODate( "2019-04-26"),
"release_date_BR": ISODate( "2019-04-25"),
"release_date_US": ISODate( "2019-04-22"),

...

}
```

Figure 2.6 Example of a document representing a movie. By applying the polymorphic model, it is possible to track the release dates of the movie in various countries.

With this model, searching by release date would require the examination of several fields at the same time. In order to search quickly, we would need several indexes on our movie collection (Figure 2.7).

```
                          Indexes

{ "release_date_IT": 1 }
{ "release_date_MX": 1 }
{ "release_date_BR": 1 }
{ "release_date _US": 1 }
```

Figure 2.7 Indexes used for release date queries.

The use of indexes certainly improves our performance when executing queries, but it can put an excessive strain on the database. In fact, each time we enter, update and/or delete data within our collection, Mongo will have to update the index structure, thus affecting the execution time of all data manipulation operations. In addition, the indexes will occupy disk and memory space when used. It is therefore advisable to use indexes only when there is a real need.

To avoid the creation of multiple indexes and avert a general performance decay, we can move the information related to the release dates in an array of sub-documents. Each subdocument will contain, for example, the country where the movie was released and the release date, as shown in the example in Figure 2.8.

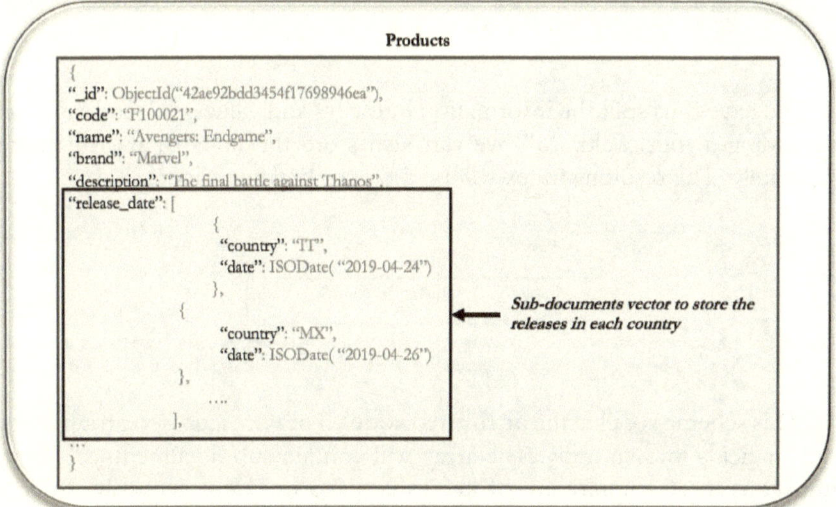

Figure 2.8 Structure of the document incorporating an array of movie release dates. The elements of the release_date array are subdocuments containing the information needed to determine both the country and the date.

Indexing becomes much more manageable because a single index can now be created on the array elements (Figure 2.9).

Figure 2.9 Definition of indexes for quick access to documents based on release country and/or date.

In a similar way, we can manage for example the dimensional characteristics of objects, such as weight, height, volume, etc. This information varies depending on the unit of measurement adopted. Therefore, we could represent the volume of a container as shown in Figure 2.10.

Specs model

```
"specs": [
    { "k": "volume", "v": "500", "u": "ml" },
    { "k": "volume", "v": "12", "u": "ounces" }
]
```

Figure 2.10 Application of the attribute model to trace the specifications of a product.

We have thus split the information into keys and values, "k" and "v", and by adding a third field, "u", we can also store the units of measurement separately. The resulting index will be the one shown in Figure 2.11.

Indexes

```
{ "specs.k": 1, "specs.v": 1, "specs.u": 1 }
```

Figure 2.11 Definition of the index for optimizing access to documents based on their characteristics.

This scheme is called the **attribute model**. The core idea is to group many similar fields into an array. The array will contain sub-documents which in turn consist, at a minimum, of key-value pairs or, more generally, share a similar structure. In addition, we can use non-deterministic field names, add additional qualifiers to the information, and more clearly outline the relationship between the original field and the value. Finally, when using the attribute model, fewer indexes are needed and, as a result, queries become easier to write and execute faster. The resulting structure is shown in Figure 2.12.

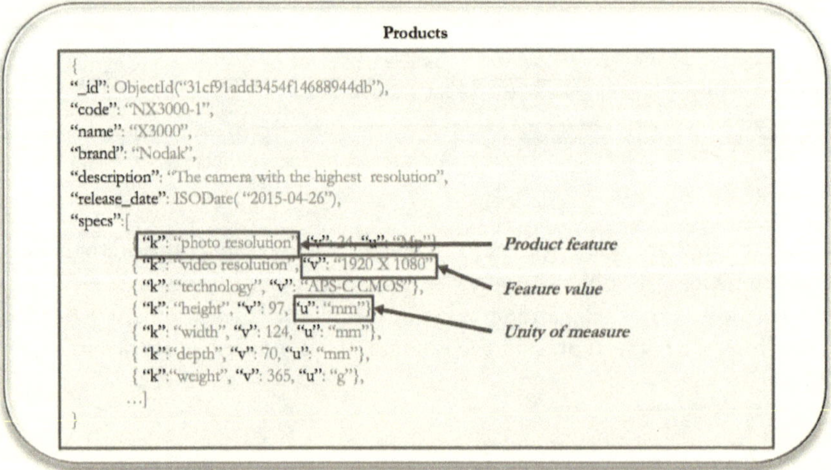

Figure 2.12 Example of a product managed with the attributes model.

2.2.1 Pros and cons of the attribute model

When a subset of fields shares common features, it can be replaced by an array of sub-documents with a structure based mainly on a key-value pair.

The schema of the subdocuments, which must have the same basic structure across the various elements of the array, can vary as needed. In this way, by defining indexes, we can query and sort documents according to these fields efficiently.

Because the model is based on a vector of elements, accessing and updating of the single element is more complex than a mere key access.

In Figure 2.13 a summary of the advantages and the disadvantages of the application of this model is provided.

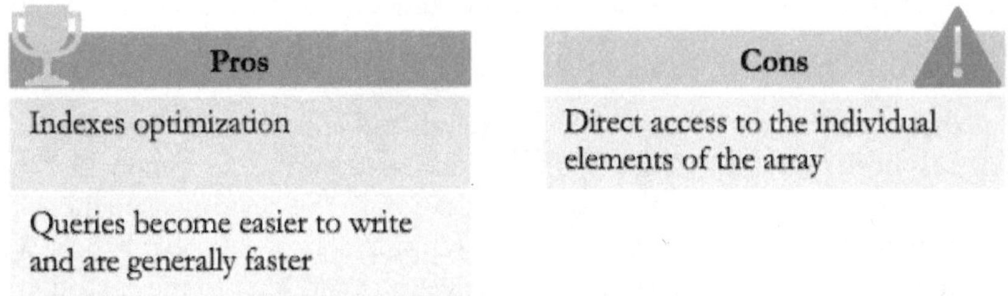

Figure 2.13 Pros and cons of the attribute model.

2.3 Extended reference model

There are situations when it is appropriate to have separate data collections. If an entity can be thought of as a separate "thing", it often makes sense to have a dedicated collection. In the case of an e-commerce application several distinct concepts exist, such as an order issued by a customer for one or more products, the customer, and the product catalog. They are all separate logical entities.

The relationship between customer and order has a one-to-many (*1-N*) cardinality. In fact, a customer can place N orders, while an order is relative to only one customer. To recover the details of an order, a JOIN operation is needed, which integrates the information from the order document with that stored in the customer document to which it refers. We should be mindful that the JOIN operation is not native to Mongo. Therefore, this operation, albeit possible thanks to the *$lookup* function of the aggregation pipeline, will have a negative impact on the performance of the application.

A possible solution is to include all the information of a customer in each order. This avoids the JOIN operation but results in the duplication of all customer data. This also introduces a consistency problem for the duplicate data. In fact, each time the customer's data is updated, the application will have to implement an appropriate strategy to make changes to the documents that include the duplicate data.

Instead of either incorporating all the customer's information in the order document, or including a reference and then performing a JOIN, we could incorporate only the fields deemed most relevant, i.e. those most frequently accessed and/or used by the application to manage an order, such as the customer's name and address. This pattern is defined as **extended reference**. It is an optimal solution when our application has to perform many repetitive JOIN operations. By identifying the most frequently accessed fields and incorporating them into the main document, performance is greatly improved.

But then, how do we select which data needs to be duplicated? As always, it depends both on the context and on data access patterns. Let us consider the receipt of an e-commerce site order. In addition to the customer's name, will we need her phone number and current shipping address? Probably not! We can then leave this data out of the order collection and refer to the customer's collection. Since the data is duplicated, this model works best if the duplicate fields do not change frequently, or their change does not affect the operation of the application. Fields such as the _id and the person's *name* are good candidates as they rarely change.

We should also take into account how any updates may affect the information related to the referenced entity, in our case the customer. Which extended references have changed? When do they need to be updated? If the information is a billing address, do we need to keep that address for historical purposes, or is it possible to update it? In some cases, the duplication of data is the best choice for maintaining historical values, a feature that can be useful in some applications. For example, it makes more sense to keep a former address, where the customer used to live at the time of product shipping, in the order document itself, and possibly retrieve the current address through the customer collection, if needed. The final model is the one shown in Figure 2.14.

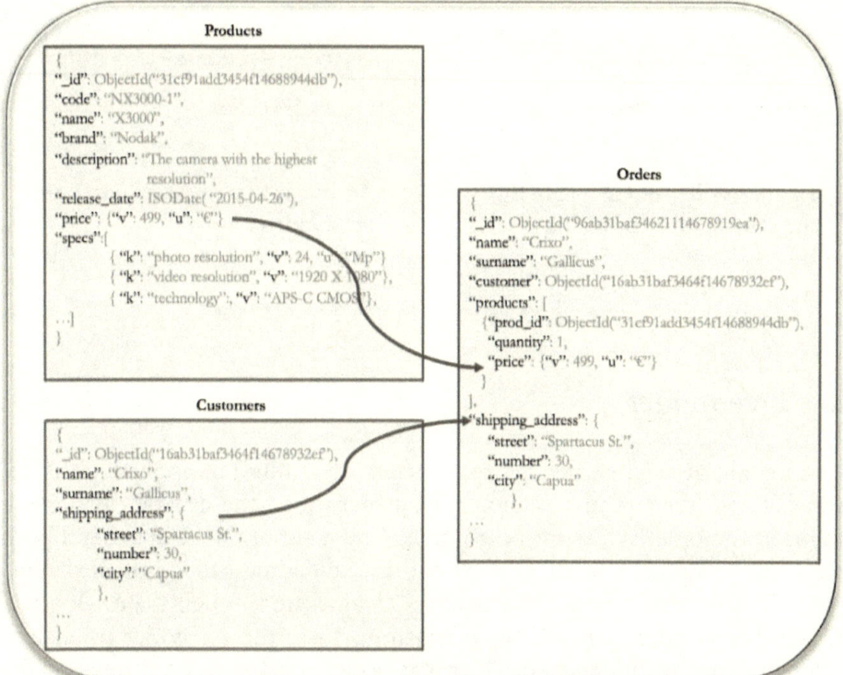

Figure 2.14 Example of including information of interest within a document of the order collection. The arrows indicate which portions of information are copied from the referenced documents of the product and customer collections.

2.3.1 Pros and cons of the extended reference model

When we need to retrieve some information frequently, we use this model to limit JOIN operations. The referencing document will contain a copy of the strictly necessary fields in the referenced one.

Duplication of data has, as a result, a disadvantage both in terms of space used and because it requires the management of updates distributed over several collections.

Figure 2.15 shows the advantages and disadvantages of using this model.

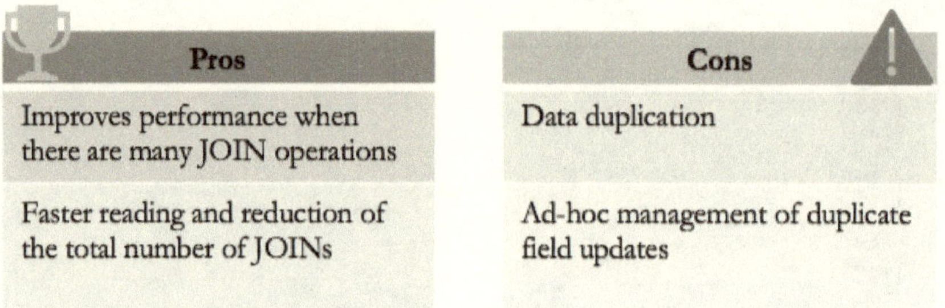

Figure 2.15 Pros and cons of the extended reference model.

2.4 Tree model

In some cases, the extended reference model cannot be applied. Consider for example the product catalog. The structure of the catalog divides the items in the online store into categories. These subdivisions are useful both from the customer's point of view and for the administrator of the online store. The customer uses the categories to navigate through the catalog and refine the product search. The administrator uses the categories to analyze sales in order to understand which categories are the most promising for applying discounts, promotional campaigns, and other marketing strategies. We can also develop additional features, such as product comparators within the same product category. Each category can also be recursively divided into subcategories. The end result is a hierarchical tree spanning the various product categories.

As we have already pointed out in Chapter 1 "A short overview of MongoDB", the time saving due to the exclusion of JOIN operations is an advantage. Therefore, we tend to group data within the same document, while duplicating some information as in the extended reference model. However, what happens if the data to be combined are hierarchical as in the example of the product categories? Mongo provides the operator *$graphLookup* to navigate the data as if they were graphs. This could be a solution. However, if we often need to query this hierarchy, the advice is to use a different data structure.

We will insert in the document a *category_hierarchy* field that will keep track of the entire hierarchy. We will also add an additional *father_category* field to store the category of the nearest parent. Duplicating this data is a good practice, especially because it still allows us to use the *$graphLookup* function on our documents. The resulting document will have the structure shown in Figure 2.16.

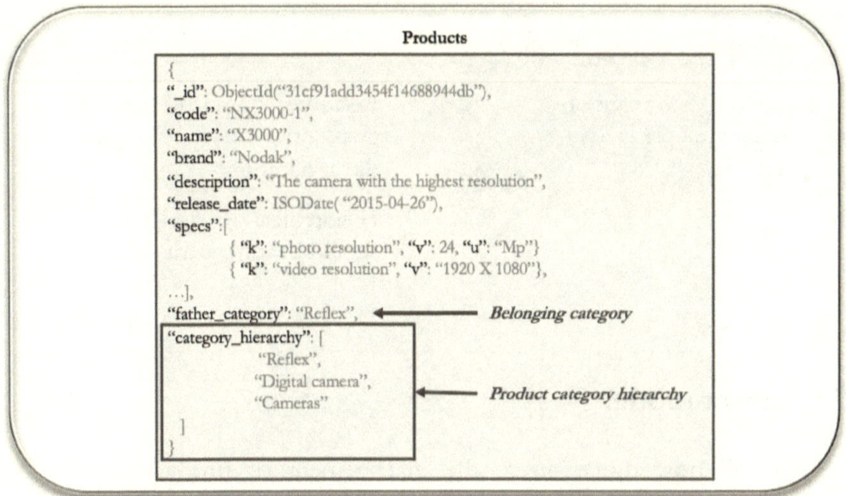

Figure 2.16 Example of managing the hierarchy of product categories.

Keeping all ancestors in an array provides the ability to create a multi-key index on those values. In this way, we can easily and quickly find all the ancestors of a given category. As for the children, these are accessible by retrieving the documents that have the category of interest as their immediate "parent".

This approach, called the **tree model**, can also be extended to graphs. Its great advantage is the increase in performance due to the elimination of multiple JOIN operations. However, graph updates, which should not be very frequent, will have to be managed by the application.

2.4.1 Pros e cons of the tree model

The tree model is a schema that is applied when data has a hierarchical or graph structure that is frequently queried. The hierarchical structure must not undergo frequent change over time.

In order to avoid the use of join operations, i.e. the use of aggregation pipelines including the *$lookup* and *$graphlookup* functions, the main document will contain an array with the elements of the hierarchical structure. The identifier of the nearest parent is usually duplicated in a separate field to easily allow hierarchy navigation operations.

The pros and cons of applying the tree model are summarized in Figure 2.17.

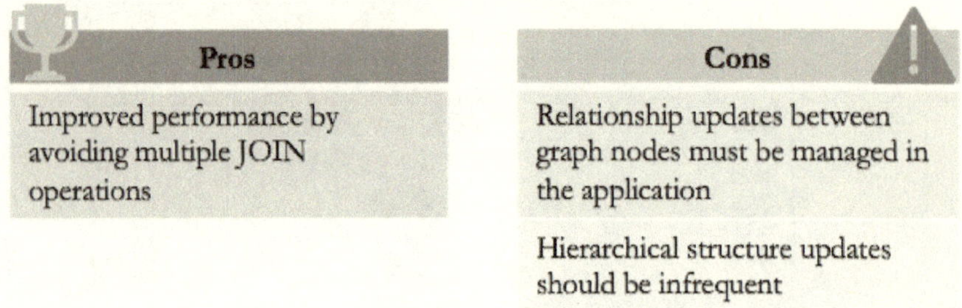

Figure 2.17 Pros e cons of the tree model.

2.5 Subset model

We will now move on to the management of product reviews by customers, a fundamental aspect of any online store. When the customer looks up a product sheet, she would like to see the most recent reviews. One possibility is to include all reviews within the product document. This would improve access time, avoiding JOIN operations, but in the long run this solution would degrade performance. In fact, Mongo keeps in the main memory the frequently accessed data, called the *working set*. When the working set exceeds the amount of RAM assigned to the DBMS, the performance degrades progressively, as the data goes is swapped out of RAM and frequent access to the disk begins to occur.

How is it possible to solve this problem? We could add more RAM to the server. This is, however, only a provisional solution that will soon become insufficient. We could think about eliminating the contents of the collection, but this will involve additional costs and complexity that the application may not be ready to meet. In some cases, this is not even actionable as a solution, as we would lose fundamental business information for our site. The only viable option is to reduce the size of our working set. When designing how to split the data, the most used part of the document should be included in the "main" collection, and the less frequently used data in another. For reviews, the criterion for this subdivision could be the number of reviews visible on the product page.

Instead of storing all reviews together with the product, we can split the collection in two. On the one hand, the collection of products will contain the most used data, e.g. current reviews; on the other hand, a second collection will include the least used data, e.g. old reviews, product history, etc. In general, when duplicating data from a one-to-many (1-N) or many-to-many (N-N) relationship, we need to analyze how the data will be queried.

The collection that most frequently requires integration with data from the referenced collection will be the optimal candidate to host the duplicate data.

For example, only the ten most recent reviews will be kept in the product collection. This allows us to reduce the working set by including only a part, or a subset, of the overall data in the product document. The additional information, i.e. all product reviews in this example, will be stored in a separate collection of Reviews that will only be accessed if the user wishes to view them (Figure 2.18).

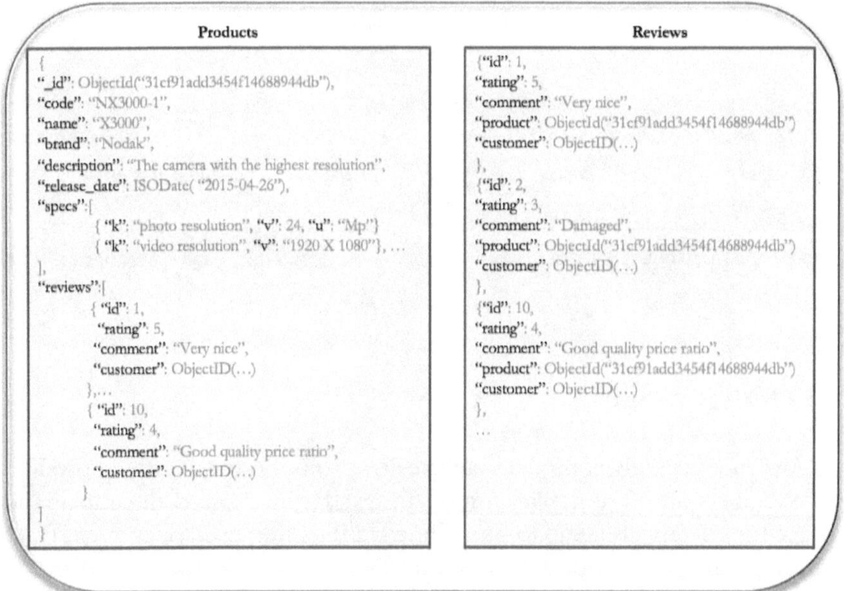

Figure 2.18 Application of the subsets pattern for review management.

This approach is known as the **subset pattern** and it is very useful when we have a large portion of data within a document, only part of which is accessed frequently. In order to limit the size of the working set, only the most significant data is included within the main document, while the remaining data are stored in a dedicated collection. We can then retrieve, for example, the most significant reviews by simply querying the collection of products. In case we need to view the reviews that are not included in our subset, we will have to issue further queries.

2.5.1 Pros and cons of the subsets model

The subset model is an option to consider when some data, which is not frequently used by the application, can cause a very significant increase in document size. This increase can significantly impact the size of the working set causing, in some cases, the RAM capacity of the computer to be exceeded.

By using smaller documents that contain the most frequently accessed data, we can reduce the overall size of the working set. This reduces disk access time for the information most often used by an application. However, the application must take on the management, selection, and update of the subset of data.

A summary of the pros and cons of this model is shown in Figure 2.19.

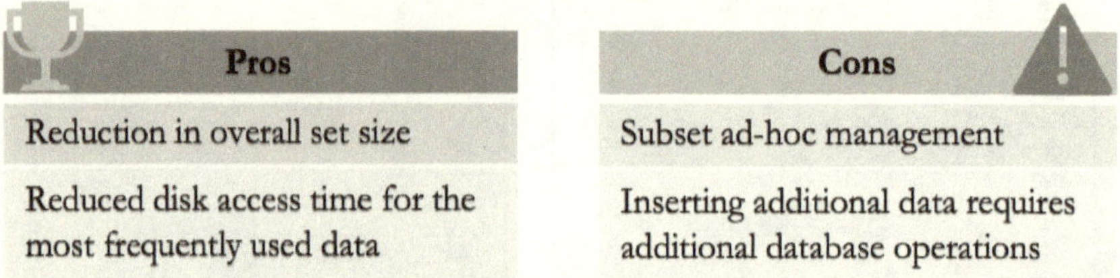

Pros	Cons
Reduction in overall set size	Subset ad-hoc management
Reduced disk access time for the most frequently used data	Inserting additional data requires additional database operations

Figure 2.19 Pros and cons of the subsets model.

2.6 Outlier model

Although the subset model is an excellent solution for managing product reviews, it requires the duplication of reviews in the product document and a logic for selecting reviews to be included in the referenced document. If we want to avoid these criticalities, we can directly insert all the reviews in the product document. This solution can be effective when, in general, each product receives few reviews.

But what happens when a product is reviewed by many users? In such cases the 16 MB size limit of the BSON document could easily be reached, which would deteriorate performance.

How can we deal with these cases? Redesigning our entire application just to address these abnormal situations could result in a performance reduction for the "normal" product, and incur an additional cost for updating the model. We must therefore manage the anomalous cases, also called outliers.

The **outlier model** is based on establishing a threshold for the maximum number of elements in the array field of interest; in addition, a new field will signal that a given document (the product, in our case study) exceeds the threshold and, therefore, is an outlier for the context.

In our example, then, a product will have the structure shown in Figure 2.20.

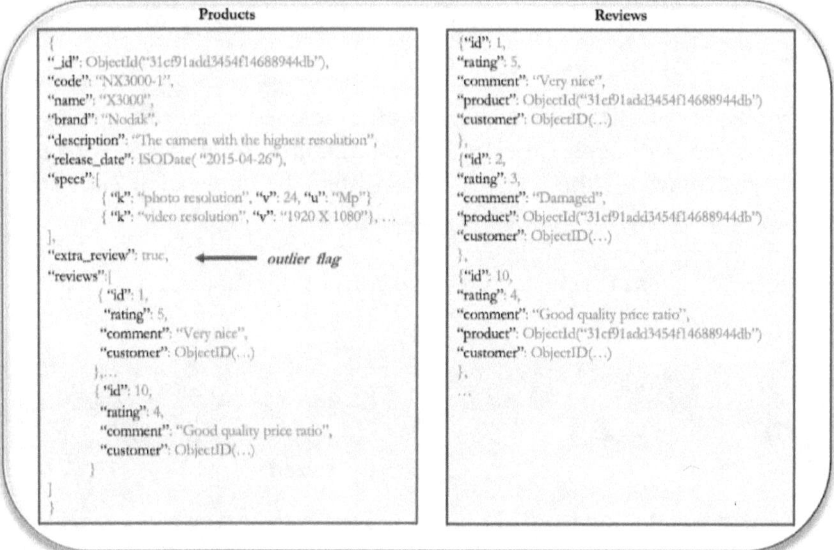

Figure 2.20 *Examples of documents belonging to the Products and Reviews collections. According to the outlier model, each Product document includes a vector with a preset number of reviews related to it. The extra_reviews field indicates if there are reviews that are not included within the document. The Reviews collection is used to save all the reviews of all products.*

We will move the excess information to a document in a separate collection and link it to the product's *_id*. Within the application, we will then be able to determine if a document has an *extra_review* field with a value equal to *true*. In that case, the application may retrieve the additional information when necessary.

The outlier model is an advanced model, which can lead to great performance improvements. It is often used in situations where the notion of popularity is an important factor, such as in social network relationships, book sales, movie reviews, etc. The Internet has turned our world into a much smaller place, and when something becomes popular, we need to change the data model around the "anomalous" object accordingly.

2.6.1 Pros and cons of the outlier model

The outliers model determines a threshold for the number of elements contained in an array. In case the document contains more than one element, we must indicate the anomaly with an additional field and save the excess information as documents in another collection, linked to the original document.

One aspect of this model is that it is often adapted to specific queries and situations. Ad-hoc queries, therefore, can result in sub-optimal performance. Also, since much of the work is done within the application code itself, additional code maintenance may be required over time.

Figure 2.21 summarizes the pros and cons of this model.

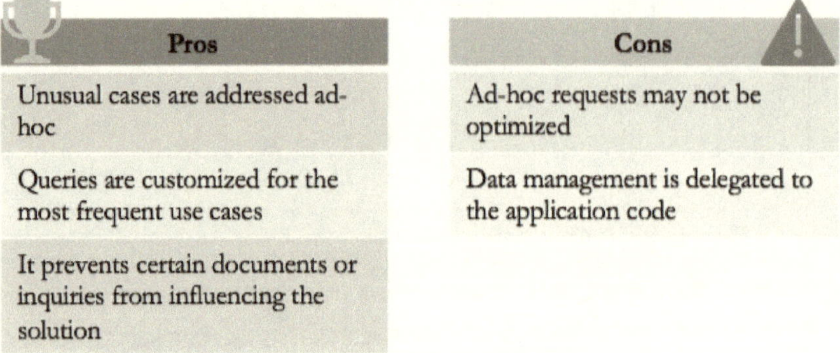

Figure 2.21 Pros and cons of the outliers' model.

2.7 What we learned

Through this case study we have addressed various aspects of modeling an e-commerce site. In general, the management of data and the way they are accessed determine the design choices of our database structure, i.e. the identification of the collections and the structure of the contained documents.

Depending on the characteristics of the data and functionalities that we wish to provide to the project, it is necessary to identify the model that offers the greatest flexibility and, at the same time, the best performance. The polymorphic model and the attribute model are certainly the most used in database development when the entities to model are heterogeneous. As a matter of fact, in addition to providing a "clean" model for the documents, they reduce the number of indexes required to improve the response time of the queries.

On the other hand, the outlier model and the subset model, which are very similar to each other, are suited to managing in an optimal way portions of data that grow with time. In this way, it is possible to retrieve the information of interest and that most frequently used, leaving the access time to the main document unchanged. Unfortunately, they require the addition of application logic to correctly manage the information that must be included in the document.

With the same goal of including only relevant information in a document, we can apply the extended reference model. Even in this case, a careful selection of the information that will be included in the referencing document will optimize read operations of the data of interest for the application.

Finally, the tree model provides a way to manage any hierarchy that must be established between different instances of an entity. However, the hierarchical structure should not undergo frequent changes, in order to avoid overloading the document update processes.

2.8 Learning checks

In the following some questions will help you evaluate the acquired knowledge. The answers can be found in Section III "Learning checks" within the chapters indicated in the "Answer" column.

Question	Answer
Assuming you have two collections for products and suppliers respectively, which model allows you to minimize read operations to extract product information integrated with that of your supplier?	Chapter 6.1
Our application manages an e-commerce site of books. Assuming we save for each book the list of all users who bought it in an array-type field, how can we manage bestsellers selling millions of copies?	Chapter 6.2
Which modeling pattern is best suited to track all product features for a comparison site?	Chapter 6.3
To speed up access to the most relevant reviews of a hotel, which model can be applied?	Chapter 6.4
Which model is more suitable to represent the organization chart of a company?	Chapter 6.5

Assuming that a company acquires over time other companies operating in different industries, which modeling pattern allows you to quickly integrate data from each new industry?	Chapter 6.6

CHAPTER 3
DESIGNING AN ENERGY CONSUMPTION MONITORING SYSTEM

The advances in the fields of electronics and wireless communication in recent years have brought to life the Internet of Things (IoT). The IoT extends the ability to collect, process, and exchange data over a network typical of computers to real-world objects, allowing for improved monitoring, control, and automation. In this way, home appliances, cameras, thermostats, factory systems, vehicles, wearable devices, and many other devices can capture information via their sensors and send it to remote servers.

The case we will analyze is related to an electricity supplier. This company has recently adopted new sensors to monitor its customers' consumption in order to obtain more detailed measurements. This data will be used for consumption-based billing as well as to detect anomalies that could indicate potential failures of the distribution lines.

After analyzing its current system for managing measurements, the company wanted to undertake a feasibility study, focusing on the use of a NoSQL database such as Mongo.

The sensors send the detected measurements through a dedicated network for security reasons. Each data packet contains some information identifying the sensor (e.g. *id_sensor*), as well as the measured parameters and the time frame in which these measurements were collected. Therefore, if the new sensors transmit power consumption measurements every minute, the data flow and the documents that will be create in the database could be as shown in Figure 3.1.

Figure 3.1 Data structure coming from the sensors.

Since we are talking about measurements over time, we can consider our data to be time series. In particular, we will explore the management of measurements and the models that can be adopted to optimize both access to the time series data and real-time analysis by operators.

3.1 Bucket model

Keeping in mind the structure of the input data, we may be inclined to store each measurement as a separate document. This model follows the relational database theory, where each record in the table represents one measurement. Unlike with relational databases, in Mongo this can pose some critical issues as the size of the data collection increases. For example, we may need to index the *id_sensor* and *timestamp* fields for each individual measurement to allow quick access. In addition, the amount of duplicate information among the documents referring to measurements of the same sensor is very high. This increases the disk space required to save our data.

One possible solution is to use the **bucket model** to group the data of the same sensor according to a certain logic.

A first possibility is to use a document for all measurements of a given sensor that are acquired in a specified time interval. This will reduce duplicate information between documents related to the same sensor (such as the *id_sensor* field), thus decreasing the space overhead required. Indexes will be optimized accordingly, allowing for simpler and more effective queries.

The document is modeled with an array of sub-documents containing the measurement of interest and the *timestamp* in which it was acquired. Other fields are usually added for optimized access in both read and write mode. For example, the *start* and *end* fields indicate the time period covered by the document, while the *n_measures* attribute is intended to store the number of objects saved in the measurement array. The resulting document is reported in Figure 3.2.

```
                           Measurements
{
  "_id": ObjectID(...),
  "id_sensor": 10001,
  "start": ISODate("2019-12-14T10:00:00.000Z"),   ⟵  start timestamp measures of the document
  "end": ISODate("2019-12-14T10:59:59.000Z"),      ⟵  end timestamp measures of the document
  "measures": [
    {
      "timestamp": ISODate("2019-12-14T10:00:00.000Z"),
      "power": 100
    },
    {
      "timestamp": ISODate("2019-12-14T10:01:00.000Z"),
      "power": 80
    },
    ...
    {
      "timestamp": ISODate("2019-12-14T10:39:00.000Z"),
      "power": 30
    }
  ],
  "n_measures": 39   ⟵  measures in the document
}
```

Figure 3.2 Application of the bucket model to the Measurements collection. Each document represents a set of measurements related to a sensor in a given time period.

The grouping logic described above, based on predetermined time slots, assumes that the number of measurements received in each time slot is almost constant. This means that the sensors need to send measurements at regular intervals, and that data losses – an indicator of possible system malfunctions – rarely occur. If these preconditions are not met, the risk, in an extreme case, is that of falling back into a situation very similar to the first scenario, where each document contains data from only one measurement. In fact, if a sensor sends only one measurement within the time interval defined by the document, the measurement vector will contain only one measurement.

In such cases, the solution is to change the grouping condition. In particular, to avoid a scattered distribution of data, a grouping based on the number of measurements received should be preferred. In this case, we will need to calculate the beginning and end of the time period each time a new measurement is entered, and increment the number of measurements stored in the *measures* array. However, this solution can manage, with the same model, sensors with different technical characteristics that could affect the data acquisition conditions. The resulting model is shown in Figure 3.3.

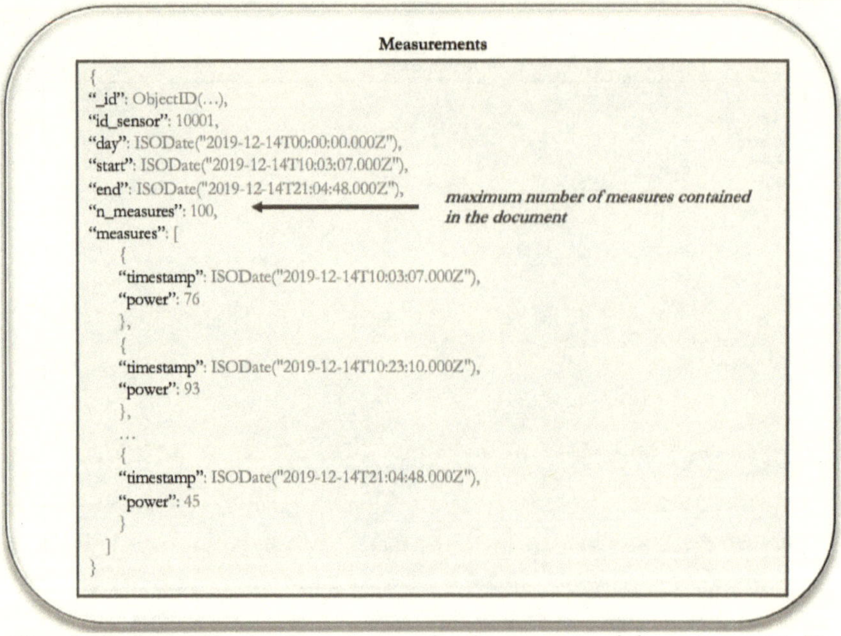

Figure 3.3 Bucket model based on the maximum number of measurements each document can contain. The start and end fields are updated according to the timestamp values of the measurement field subdocuments.

3.1.1 Pros and cons of the bucket model

The bucket model is an excellent solution when we need to manage streaming data such as time series, real-time analysis or Internet of Things (IoT) applications.

Depending on the application context, the best data grouping strategy should be defined in order to reduce the number of documents required for tracking. The management of groups of measures and the creation of new documents is left to the application. Used in combination with the pre-aggregated value model, which we will see later, it is an optimal solution to provide accurate statistics with minimum resources.

Figure 3.4 shows the advantages of using this approach.

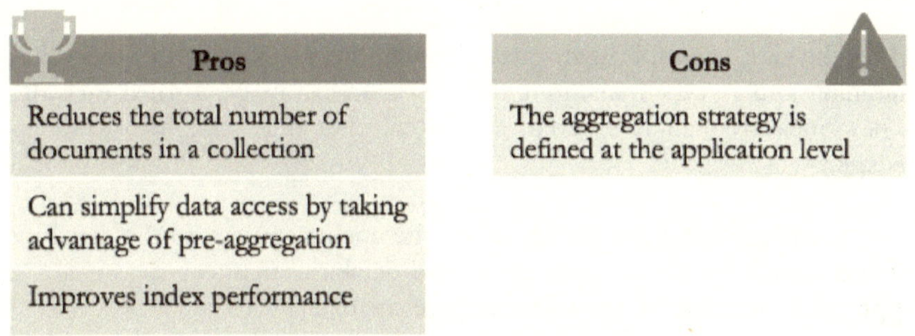

Figure 3.4 Pros and cons of the buckets model

3.2 Pre-aggregated value model

The bucket model largely solves the management of time series, but it leaves to the application the calculation of the aggregate measures that are usually needed by users analysing the series data. Examples of aggregate measures are represented by the average over a time interval and the minimum and maximum values recorded in that period. Performing these calculations every time they are requested, especially when handling large amounts of data, can be very expensive, as it can require many CPU cycles, high disk access and increased main memory usage.

In many cases, however, it is not necessary to know the exact, real-time value of the aggregate measures. We could therefore perform calculations in the background and update the document with the calculated measures accordingly. The stored values provide a valid representation of the data without the need for further calculations. This model is called **pre-aggregated value** pattern.

The logic with which the aggregate measures are updated obviously depends on the application context. In general, since we are not interfering with the source data, we may repeat the calculation at any time without affecting the validity of the result. In a context where writes to the database occur with a low frequency, the calculation can be done in combination with any update of the source data. Where more regular writes are present, calculations could be performed at defined intervals (e.g. every hour). Other strategies for performing the calculation could include, for example, adding a timestamp to the document to indicate when the aggregate measures were last updated. Thus, the application can determine when the calculation should be performed again. Another option could be to create a queue of tasks, each calculating certain aggregate measures, to be performed in asynchronous mode.

In the case of simple aggregate measures, such as the sum of the values, the minimum and the maximum, the operation can be performed each time a new measurement is entered, as the calculation is straightforward and inexpensive.

It is advisable to leave the choice of the update strategy to the developer of the application, while it is up to the database architect to prepare an appropriate structure to contain the aggregate data.

Measurements

```
{
"_id": ObjectID(...),
"id_sensor": 10001,
"start": ISODate("2019-12-14T10:00:00.000Z"),
"end": ISODate("2019-12-14T10:59:59.000Z"),
"measures": [
    {
    "timestamp": ISODate("2019-12-14T10:00:00.000Z"),
    "power": 100
    },
    ...
    {
    "timestamp": ISODate("2019-12-14T10:39:00.000Z"),
    "power": 30
    }
  ],
"n_measures": 39
"tot_power": 2452        ←——— pre-aggregated measure
}
```

Figure 3.5 The tot_power field represents the aggregate calculation (the sum) of all measurements in the document. By using aggregates, we can quickly calculate some statistical data.

Back to the previous example, we could add a pre-aggregated *tot_power* value that stores the sum of the measurements contained in our document (Figure 3.5). At this point the average energy consumption over the time interval defined by the document can be simply computed as the ratio between *tot_power* and *n_measures*. Therefore, using pre-aggregated measures we can efficiently answer many frequently asked questions without overloading the DBMS.

In general, the calculation of pre-aggregated attributes is used in the case where a subset of data must be recomputed frequently by our application, or when the data access pattern is read-intensive. For example, if we have 1,000,000 reads but only 1,000 writes per hour, updating measurements at the time of each write would reduce the number of calculations by a factor of 1000.

3.2.1 Pros and cons of the pre-aggregated values model

When the application has very read-intensive data access patterns and these data have to be repeatedly recalculated, the pre-aggregated value model is an excellent option to explore. However, care must be taken not to abuse it in order not to overload the system when entering and updating information.

Figure 3.6 shows the advantages and disadvantages introduced by this model.

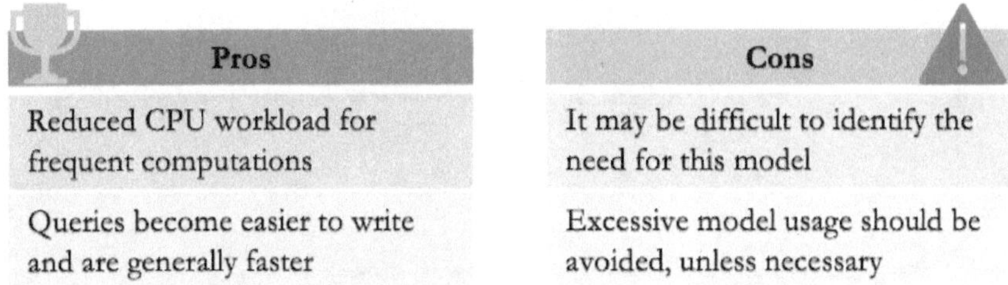

Figure 3.6 Pros and cons of the pre-aggregated values model

3.3 Approximation model

As we have seen, pre-aggregated values provide an excellent tool to quickly calculate statistics on a portion of data contained in a document. However, if the need arises to aggregate several documents, the calculation may become expensive.

For example, if we wanted our application to show a customer's energy consumption, we would potentially need to aggregate several sensors and/or multiple measurements over time. Therefore, we should evaluate whether, within the application context, this information should be provided with high accuracy, or if an approximation could suffice.

In case an approximation is sufficient, how can we represent it in the database? One option is to create an attribute that contains the result of the approximate calculation within a document used to hold statistics. In our case, we could use a document for each customer, which represents a consumption report in a specific time interval (Figure 3.7).

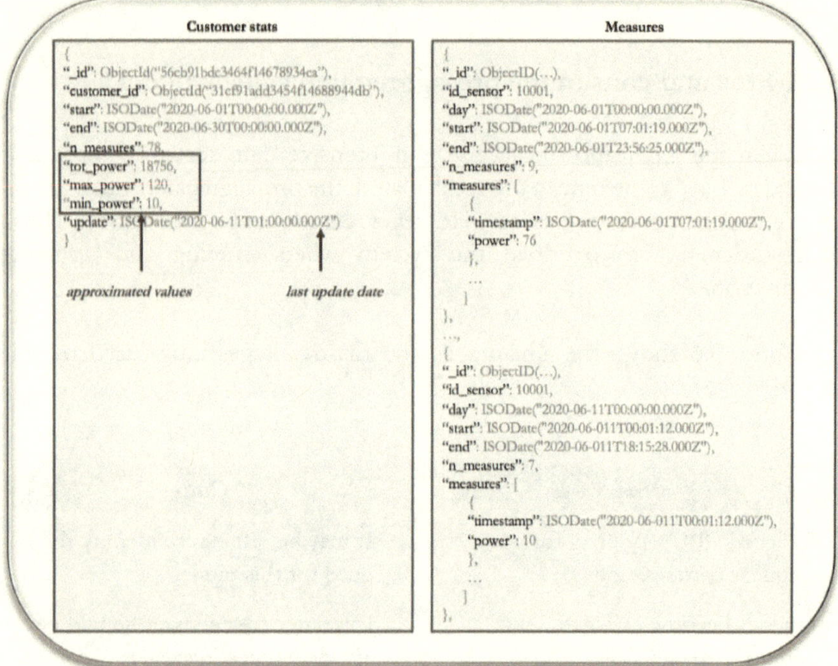

Figure 3.7 Documents in the Customer statistics collection contain an approximation of the energy consumption statistics. Note that, in this case, the update took place on June 11, 2020 at the beginning of the day, while raw measurements are available until the evening of the same day.

This way we won't have to calculate our statistics every time we receive a measurement, but we will always have a fairly reliable estimate of this information. This approach is called the **approximation model**.

When is this methodology useful? It is typically used when we need to display aggregated information on data whose computation calls for very high computational resources (time, memory, CPU cycles), but we do not require extreme accuracy or real-time up-to-dateness.

In our example, do energy consumption statistics (average, maximum, minimum) require high accuracy? Does the calculation of these statistics take a long time compared to the arrival of new measurements? Would a minimal change in the computed statistics have a significant impact on the usage and functionality of the application?

With our application scenario in mind, we can define an approximation factor that allows us to write only few times to our database, all the while providing statistically significant data. If, for example, this information is used to feed a consumption monitoring system for our customers, the real-time variation of this information will most likely not be a priority for the end user, who will be more interested in the overall consumption value, with a certain amount of tolerance.

The strategy to be adopted within the application will have to take into account the number of updates to a customer's consumption data. When the number of updates reaches a fixed threshold, the estimated values will be recomputed. Let's suppose we set a threshold of 100 measurements. With this strategy, our statistics will be updated only once every hundred measurements received. We have thus reduced the number of writes to the database by about 99%.

The conditions under which the procedure for calculating the approximate values is carried out can vary. They are subjected to an analysis of the data flow and the acceptable tolerance for the accuracy of the estimated values. For example, we may create a function that returns a random integer number in a range between 0 and N. Each time this function returns 0, the calculation of the estimated values will be performed. This will result in a reduction of about $1/N\%$ of the number of writes.

3.3.1 Pros and cons of the approximation model

The usage of this methodology comes to our rescue when working with large amounts of data or a large number of users, and the impact on the performance of the write operations can be considerable. By reducing both the number of writes and the resources allocated to data that does not require high accuracy, we can certainly benefit from significant improvements in database performance.

The criticality of this model, however, lies in the fact that the exact statistics are not provided in real time and the implementation of update policies is left to the application itself. Finally, it can only be applied when the calculations to be made are very expensive and their accuracy is not a priority.

A summary of the pros and cons of this model is shown in Figure 3.8.

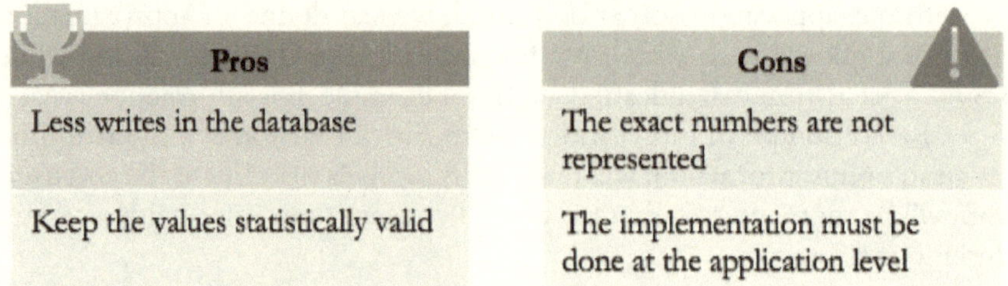

Pros	Cons
Less writes in the database	The exact numbers are not represented
Keep the values statistically valid	The implementation must be done at the application level

Figure 3.8 Pros and cons of the approximation model

3.4 What we learned

Time series management is one of the most interesting topics of our days. In this chapter we have seen how to use a document database to efficiently manage the large amount of data that can be generated by IoT sensors.

The modeling patterns analyzed can be reused in other areas, where time series are the focus of the context of interest. For example, a financial context, where we need to monitor stock trends, is similar to the one described. The same applies to tools that analyze network traffic with the aim of detecting malicious attacks, or simply to provide statistics on the popularity and use of websites.

By combining the various models, it is possible to optimize both resource usage and query execution times. In addition, applications can provide statistics of interest with a low latency, with an accuracy that depends on the model applied.

By taking advantage of Mongo's features, we can also reduce the space occupied by our database on disk. Indeed, in the field of time series, keeping obsolete data it is not always necessary, especially when they have already been processed and their aggregate measures have been saved properly. Removing such data can be useful for reducing disk space and improving the performance of our database.

There are several strategies. Among them, the one that exploits the data model seen previously, with a low implementation cost, is the use of Time-To-Live (TTL) indices.

TTLs, unlike normal indexes, are defined with an associated time interval, whose expiry causes the deletion of indexed documents in a given collection. In our example we could therefore create a TTL index on the *end* field that will delete documents older than a week, using the command shown in Figure 3.9.

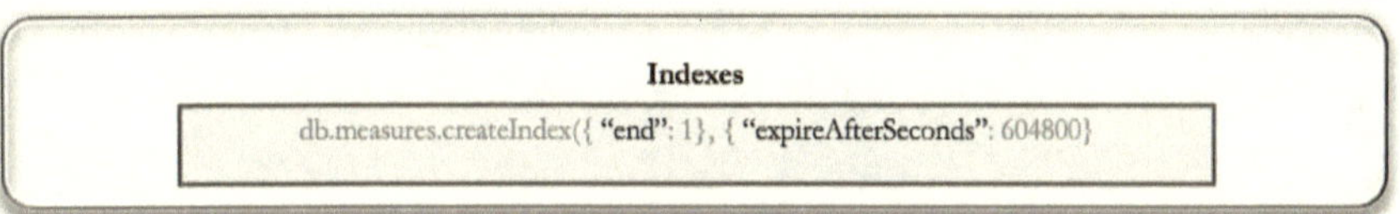

Figure 3.9 Time-To-Live (TTL) index to automatically delete measurements older than a week.

By combining the model seen above with a TTL index, our database will contain only the most recent measurement data, but it will be able to provide meaningful statistics without any loss of information.

3.5 Learning checks

In the following we provide some questions to evaluate the acquired knowledge. The answers can be found in Section III "Learning checks" within the chapters indicated in the "Answer" column.

Question	Answer
Which model may be applied for saving thousands of log entries generated by different information systems?	Chapter 6.7
In the modeling of a civil registry database, which pattern could improve the performance of generating population distribution statistics?	Chapter 6.8
Which strategies and models can be applied to streamline our database storing measurements from different devices?	Chapter 6.9
Supposing we wish to monitor network traffic on various websites, which aggregation strategy is the most effective when using the bucket model?	Chapter 6.10
To the aim of minimizing resource consumption and database writes, which patterns may be used to compute performance scores in an IoT system?	Chapter 6.11

CHAPTER 4
DESIGNING AN INFORMATION SYSTEM FOR A MEDICAL CENTER

As our last case study, we will look at a more niche context, whose issues may nonetheless be of interest in other areas. We want to manage and update a medical center database used by an application for managing medical examinations and their related documents. A prototype with limited functionality has already been developed based on Mongo, so we will focus on updating it and adding new features. In order to provide a fully-functional platform within the immediate future, it is necessary to complete the available prototype with the missing functionality, i.e. that of the examination reservation.

The new required functionality is related to the clinic reservation. Each clinic is available on certain days of the week and at set times. Some clinics may not be available in certain time slots. The application will need to store the booked examinations at each clinic and provide a quick and intuitive view of their occupancy.

The initial prototype manages the electronic patient records. Some personal data and telephone contacts are tracked for each patient. During the development of the new application, we should evaluate whether the model currently used to store the patients' personal information meets the needs of the medical center.

Some experimental clinical trials are conducted at the medical center. To participate in a clinical trial, the patient must sign an informed consent form for authorizing or denying the use of the data and the biological samples collected by the medical center. The patient has the right, at any time, to modify the authorizations given. For legal reasons, the database will have to track the various modifications of the consents.

Below, we will analyze the models that make it possible to properly manage the new functionalities and support the evolution of the application.

4.1 Preallocation model

To implement the required booking functionality, we need to deal with the problem of managing the time slots of the visits and the dedicated clinic spaces. In particular, we need our application to identify a free clinic in a specific time slot in a simple and intuitive way. A two-dimensional representation of the problem can help us with this. One dimension will represent the time slots within a working day, while the other will list the clinics. The cell value, if present, will contain the code of the booked visit, indicating that the clinic is not available at that time. Otherwise, we may allocate the clinic to a new visit. Figure 4.1 shows an example of the representation used.

Monday 2020-06-01	Room A	Room B	Room C
09:00-10:00	V00001		A00002
10:00-11:00	A00008	V00002	
11:00-12:00			C00004
14:00-15:00	V00007		
15:00-16:00		C00001	A00005
16:00-17:00	C00005		C00006

Figure 4.1 Matrix representation of clinic usage on a working day.

But how can we represent a matrix structure like the one shown in Figure 4.1 within the database? Although Mongo provides flexibility in the document structure, in some cases a fixed document structure can be very useful. The case we are analyzing introduces the **preallocation pattern**. Through this model, we can represent the availability matrix of the clinics as a two-dimensional array where, for example, each cell is associated with a "time" and a "room" (Figure 4.2). It is also possible to represent the unavailability of some clinics at certain times by excluding from the two-dimensional array the combinations that are not available. It will then be easy to write an application that is able to analyze the two-dimensional array and identify a free room at a certain time, without resorting to complex formulas.

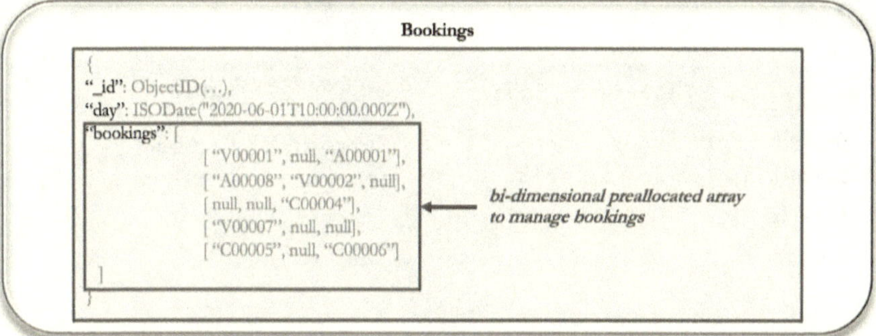

Figure 4.2 Example of a preallocated structure for the reservation of clinics.

This solution therefore requires creating an empty initial structure, which will be filled later. It may seem trivial, but it is necessary to balance the desired result in terms of simplification against the additional resources that the solution may require. Larger documents will make the working set larger, resulting in more RAM needed to accommodate it. The application code will be easier to write and maintain, but care must be taken so that the request for memory does not exceed the available RAM.

Preallocation was a popular pattern in Mongo versions prior to 3.2, which used MMAPv1 as their storage engine. However, this engine performed best when documents did not grow in size over time. When a document grew in size, it had to be relocated to a different disk block. This operation was very expensive and consequently slowed down the database. Starting with Mongo version 3.2, with the use of WiredTiger and the deprecation of MMAPv1, the preallocation model lost much of its importance. Nevertheless, as we have seen, in some contexts it can be useful for an optimal and efficient data management.

4.1.1 Pros and cons of the preallocation model

When the structure of the document is known and the application simply needs to fill it with data, the preallocation model is the right choice, because the document structure is defined a priori, and its modeling is very simple. Unfortunately, this model does not take advantage of the full potential of the

WiredTiger engine, thus decreasing the overall performance.

Finally, the final schema will be rigid and, therefore, unsuitable to evolving the data structure. For this reason, its use should be carefully evaluated. Figure 4.3 shows the advantages and disadvantages of this model.

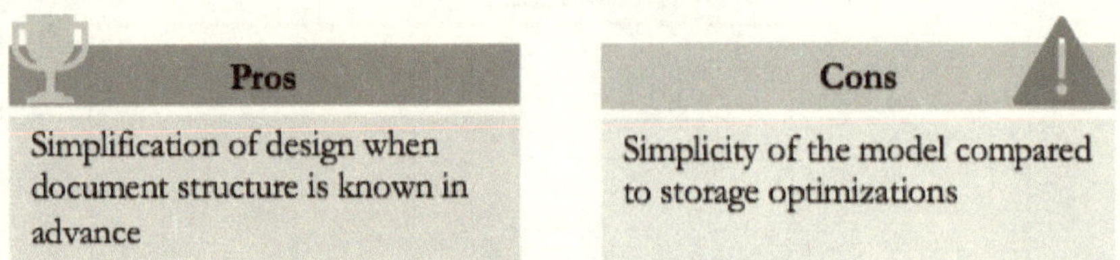

Figure 4.3 Pros and cons of the preallocation model.

4.2 Document versioning model

Another functionality required by the new application is the management of informed consent updates, i.e. those documents that authorize the medical center to manage personal data, collected biological material and laboratory results for scientific and/or statistical studies. These documents do not vary greatly over time and are relatively few, as they relate to certain studies that are performed by the center. In addition, only the latest version of the document is of interest, while the others are maintained for historical/legal purposes. We can therefore apply a solution called **document versioning**.

This model consists in maintaining a versioning history of available and usable documents. In addition, it allows us to manage document revisions within our database, without having to resort to external versioning systems.

The model is based on adding a field to each document that keeps track of the document version. The database will have two collections: the first one contains the latest version of the documents and, hence, the most frequently requested data, whilst the second stores all revisions of the data. An example is shown in Figure 4.4.

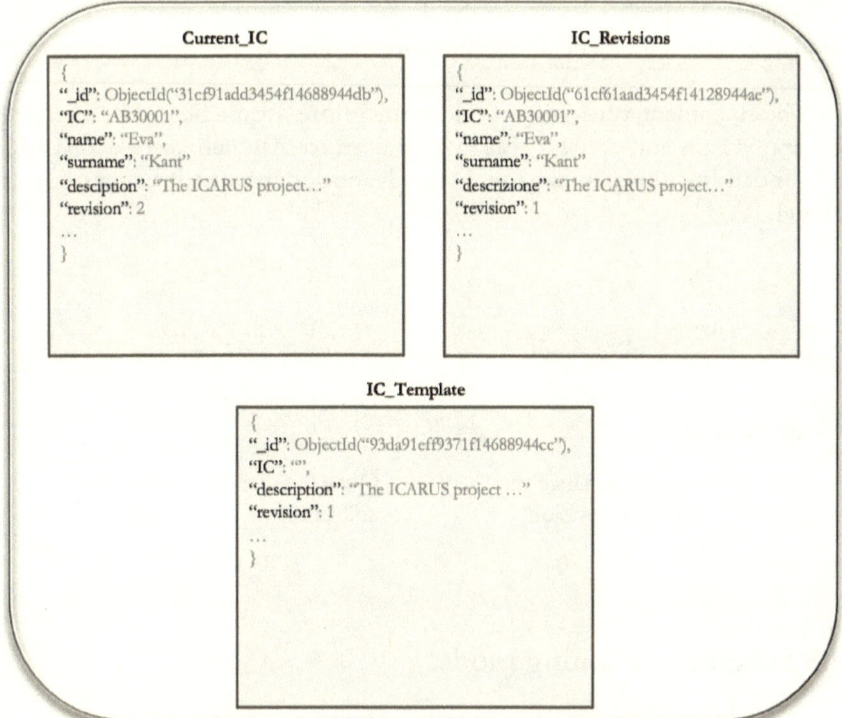

Figure 4.4 *Collections for the management of informed consent (IC) through the document versioning pattern. The IC_Template collection is used as a basic structure for the documents to be inserted.*

But when can Document Versioning be applied? As in the previous cases, it is essential to analyze the characteristics of the data to be tracked and the data access patterns followed by the application. In the case of Document Versioning, it is required that each entity of interest should not have too many revisions and that the number of instances should be contained. Moreover, it is essential that the most frequent queries are made on the latest version, while the history must be retrieved only in special and rare cases.

4.2.1 Pros and cons of the document versioning model

The document versioning model is relatively simple to implement. It can be implemented on existing systems without heavily changing the application or the existing documents. In addition, the performance of queries accessing the latest version of the document is never affected.

The disadvantages of this model are the need to access a different collection of historical information, and a higher number of writes, due to maintaining multiple versions of the documents. For this reason, one of the fundamental requirements is that updates are not too frequent.

The document versioning model is therefore a possible solution when, for application and context reasons, we need to maintain all revisions of a document. Figure 4.5 summarizes the advantages and disadvantages of this model.

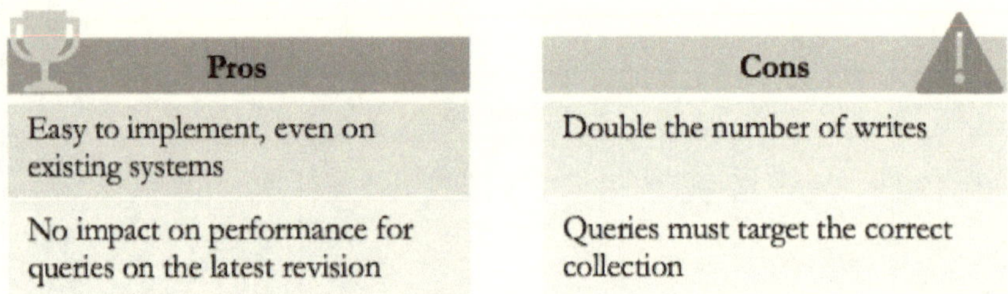

Figure 4.5 Pros and cons of the document versioning model.

4.3 Schema versioning model

Let's suppose now that, after a certain period of time, the medical center requires an update of the application, as it has become necessary to trace new data. This is a very frequent case in any information system. Obviously, we will need to study the new use cases, the data that we want to trace, and how to access the data, in order to identify the most suitable representation model.

But how can we implement changes to both the code and the database without the risk of compromising the overall software operation? Our choice of using Mongo from the beginning of the project brings us a big advantage, compared to a solution based on relational databases. Indeed, updating the structures of a relational database is very challenging, as it requires redefining the existing table structures and/or possibly insert new portions of databases with additional structures (indexes). In addition, the migration of data from the previous schema to the current one must be envisioned, not always a simple and error-free operation. The software functionalities affected by the changes to the database must be subsequently rewritten. This requires that, at a certain moment, the service be interrupted to perform the migration of both data and software. In some contexts, such an interruption can cause damage to the customer. Finally, what happens if the new version does not meet the customer's expectations? Returning to the old version can be a much worse nightmare.

But what advantages does Mongo bring compared to relational databases? We can use the **schema versioning** pattern. This pattern takes full advantage of the polymorphism feature of Mongo collections, which we have already used earlier in the book. How do we modify the application so that we can manage multiple versions of the documents? One possibility is to check the presence and/or value of the *schema_version* field. This field will allow our application to know how to manage the document at hand. For example, we can assume that documents without this field are version 1. Each new schema release would increase the value of the *schema_version* field, so that the schema could be treated accordingly by the application.

The new information to be inserted in the document will be saved using the structure of the latest version. Based on the context, we could update all documents to the new version by default, or we could defer the update until the time of the first write access.

Going back to our example, let's suppose that the medical center realizes it needs to track multiple methods of contacting its patients. The initial template used by the application only included a couple of contact details, as shown in the example in Figure 4.6.

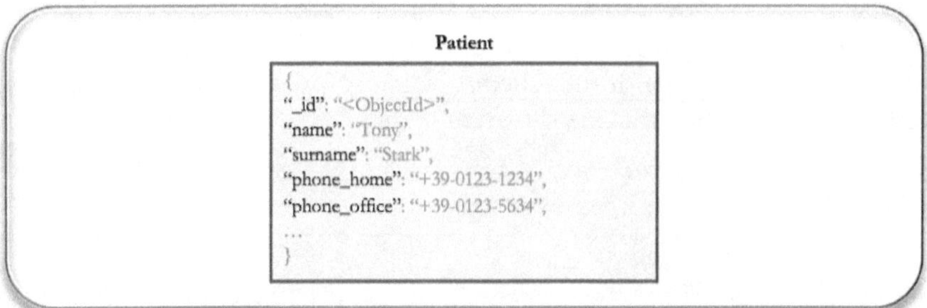

Figure 4.6 Original model of a Patient document.

A first adjustment that we propose to the medical center is to add some fields to the model in order to store new contact methods. The model will then become as shown in Figure 4.7.

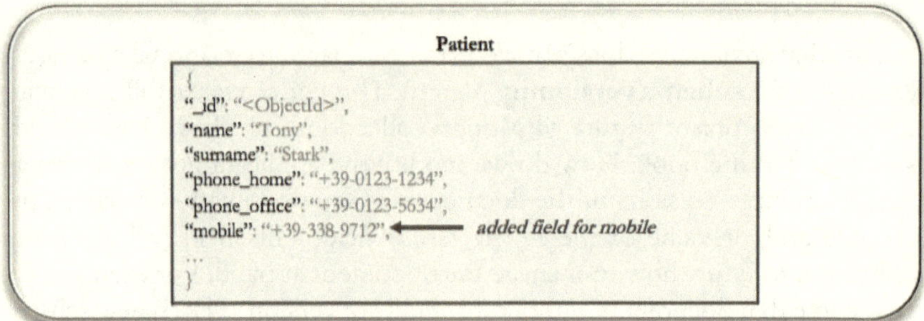

Figure 4.7 New fields were added to the original model to comply with the new functional specifications.

This change does not require the use of the versioning pattern, since we simply added fields that do not affect our functions. However, during the testing period of the new release of the application, the medical center informs us that their patients do not always have the same contact methods, so the data input and display strategy we designed is inadequate. Thus, we try to move to a leaner version, both at the user interface and the database level, which will guard us against the generation of any new contact methods that may arise in the future.

A solution could make use of the attribute model that we have exploited when designing the e-commerce site. We must therefore change the structure of the document by adding a *contacts* field containing a vector of sub-documents, each representing a contact method. Since we are significantly modifying the structure of the schema, we must use schema versioning. The resulting document is the one shown in Figure 4.8.

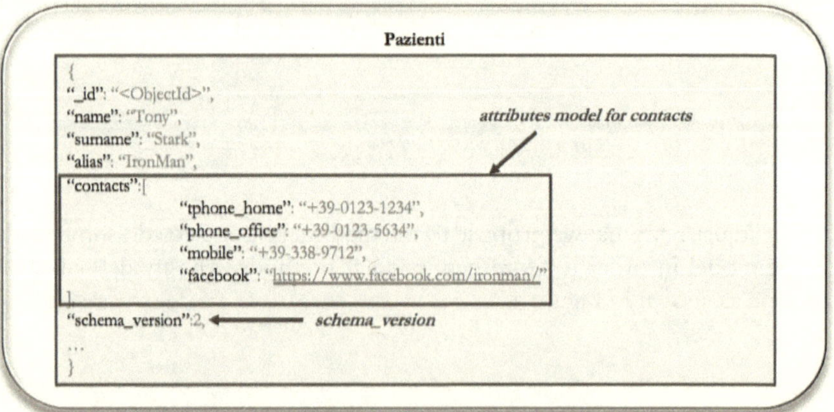

Figure 4.8 Updating the scheme with the insertion of a sub-document vector to track all possible contact modes for a patient.

4.3.1 Pros and cons of the schema versioning model

The enormous advantage of this approach is that the various changes can be made without database downtime. By properly designing our application, we could read documents belonging to both versions of the schema. In addition, it is possible to minimize, or even eliminate, application downtime through appropriate strategies.

Almost all applications can benefit from the schema versioning model, as changes to the data schema often occur during the life cycle of an application. This model allows previous and current versions of documents to coexist in a collection. The advantages and disadvantages of using this model are shown in Figure 4.9.

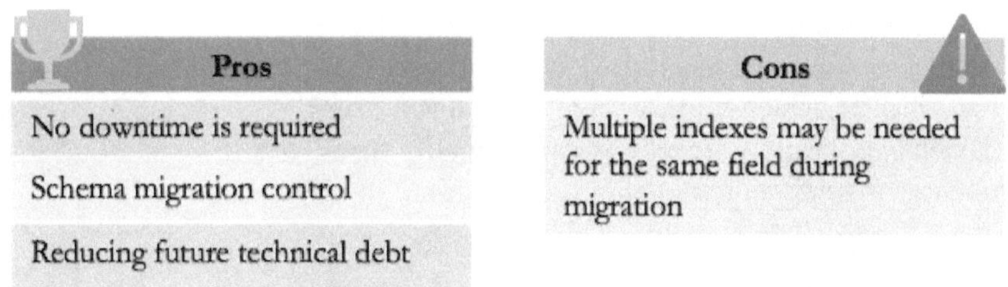

Figure 4.9 Pros and cons of the schema versioning model.

4.4 What we learned

This last example, related to an information system and its management over time, has allowed us to delve into scenarios that may occur in countless other contexts. In particular, we analyzed how to model the use of spaces over time, but especially how to update documents and diagrams without compromising the normal operation of the application.

The advantage of a NoSQL supporting polymorphism is especially evident in that it helps developers to keep applications updated, adapt them to new requirements and minimize possible inefficiencies related to the release of new versions.

Versioning models, both for documents and schema, can be adopted in any application context. Their ductility makes them the best choice to help designers and developers deal with constantly evolving projects.

The pre-allocation model, as mentioned above, has lost its strengths with the use of the WiredTiger engine. However, it is a pattern to consider in certain contexts where modeling can simplify data management, and systems are not particularly overloaded.

4.5 Learning checks

In the following some questions are proposed to evaluate the acquired knowledge. The answers can be found in Section III "Learning checks" within the chapters indicated in the "Answer" column.

Question	Answer
Which storage engine benefits from the pre-allocation model?	Chapter 5.6
To avoid service interruptions during a database schema update, which model is most convenient?	Chapter 6.12
Assuming you need to model a seat reservation system for a theater, which modeling pattern can you use?	Chapter 6.13
Which application scenario can benefit from the document versioning model?	Chapter 6.14

SECTION III
LEARNING CHECKS

CHAPTER 5
THEORY QUESTIONS

In this chapter you will find some questions and answers to test your understanding of the theory topics covered in the chapters of Section II "Case Studies".

5.1 Polymorphism

What does polymorphism allow?

One of the great advantages of NoSQL databases is fact of being schemaless, i.e. the lack of a predefined schema. Documental databases, including Mongo, take advantage of this feature to introduce the concept of polymorphism. This aspect allows us to create documents belonging to the same collection but with different data structures. In this way, we can track specific information for the documents that need it, without having to create additional collections or complex data structures.

As seen in Chapter 2 "Designing an e-commerce website", the polymorphism-based model allows us to create a single collection for e-commerce products. Each document will contain some information shared by all products, but it may also include fields that are specific to the individual product. This pattern can also be applied to subdocuments to make the model more expressive and flexible.

5.2 Atomicity in MongoDB

How and when can atomicity be guaranteed on multiple documents in Mongo?

Atomicity means that a database operation cannot be decomposed into sub-processes. A write operation, therefore, will be consolidated to the database if, and only if, no errors occur during its execution.

In MongoDB, write operations are atomic if, and only if, they affect only one document. Conversely, in relational databases, atomicity is guaranteed both at the single-record level and at the table level.

When we need to guarantee atomicity on several operations, we must create transactions. This concept has long been present in relational databases, while it has only been introduced in MongoDB since version 4.0, but limited to replica set configurations. From version 4.2, transactions may be used even with sharded configurations. Thanks to the introduction of transactions, it is possible to guarantee the atomicity of operations spanning several documents, even belonging to different collections.

5.3 NoSQL Features

What are the main features of NoSQL databases?

Each NoSQL database has some unique features. The common ones are:
- Schemaless
- Non-relational
- Scalability

These features make it possible to develop models capable of adapting to the changing needs that may arise during the software life cycle. In addition, they can aptly represent the interconnections between the data through special structures, different from the relational ones. The scalability of NoSQL technologies allows developers to make the best use of available computational resources, slowing down the demand for more and more powerful machines.

5.4 Analysis in MongoDB

Which Mongo function can be used to analyze the data saved in a collection or to integrate information from different collections?

Analyzing the data stored in a database is essential to any activity. For data scientists, extracting up-to-date statistics is the first step to advanced analysis. A very common solution – not only with MongoDB – is to create (possibly very complex) queries that calculate the measures of interest. In relational databases this approach is among the most common.

Another possibility borrowed from the world of relational databases is to create a data warehouse that is fed through ETL processes (Extract, Transform, Load) with aggregated data. This type of approach allows different analyses to be performed on dedicated databases, separate from the procedural ones. Despite this, there is often a need for additional resources both to perform ETL processes and to save the aggregated data.

Even though the JOIN operation is not native to Mongo, the pipeline aggregation was introduced in the latest versions in order to avoid the use of data warehouses. This feature allows us to create pipelines for multiple purposes. For example, we can extract documents of interest, transform data structures, merge information from the same or different collections, group documents according to specific criteria, calculate aggregate measurements, and much more.

The commands described in this text for integrating information from different documents are *$graphLookup* and *$lookup*. The former allows for recursive navigation between documents, while the latter performs a left outer join.

5.5 NoSQL for Social Networks

What types of NoSQL databases can be used to model a social network?

To answer this question, it is necessary to initially analyze the context of social networks in order to identify the types of data that the database will need to manage and the functionalities that the application will implement.

To date, everyone knows, and many of us also use, different social networks such as Facebook, Twitter, LinkedIn, Tinder, etc. Each of these has been mainly developed to connect users from different locations around the world who share common interests and/or experiences.

For example, Facebook, created at Harvard in the United States by Mark Zuckerberg and his friends, was originally designed to share names and photos of university students with the aim of facilitating socialization among students. The enormous success changed many aspects and much of the functionality of the original platform. However, even today, the main reason for enrollment for a large number of users is to stay in touch with old and new friends, sharing their personal experiences and ideas.

On the other hand, LinkedIn was born to provide a digital platform for users to publish their work experiences, look for jobs, and enlarge the circle of potential customers.

The common factor in these examples is the creation of a social network that connects different individuals. The technology that best fits each scenario should be identified based on this salient aspect.

The database should primarily host user data and the connections that will be established among them. For this reason, an abstract model of a social network uses a graph representation, as shown in Figure 5.1. The nodes, or vertices, of the graph represent the users, while the arcs that join two nodes describe a relationship between two users.

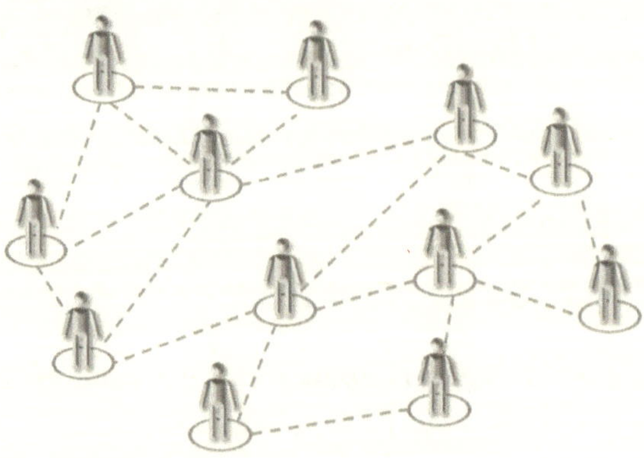

Figure 5.1 A graph representation of a social network.

Starting from this abstract modeling, the most immediate choice is a NoSQL graph database. These databases build upon graph theory to perform optimized searches on tree and/or graph structures. In addition, they can save the characteristics of nodes and arcs using a key-value pair model. The most used commercial database belonging to this category is currently Neo4j [7].

Although this type of database is the most suitable to model a social network, it suffers from some limitations, when searches are not based on graph navigation. For example, searching for all nodes with certain characteristics can be very slow and expensive, if the graph is large and/or no secondary supporting structures, such as indexes, have been created.

A possible alternative is to use document databases, especially MongoDB.

Through the aggregation pipeline, with the *$graphLookup* function, it is possible to navigate the various documents that are mutually referenced, as if they represented a graph. Obviously, every single document, which represents a user, must contain the list of his first level contacts. In Figure 5.2 an example of a model for a social network user is shown.

User

```
{
"_id": "iron_man",
"name": "Tony",
"surname": "Stark",
"friends":["captain_america", "black_widow", "hulk"]
...
}
```

Figure 5.2 Example of the structure of a document for a social network user.

At the modeling level, therefore, MongoDB is also a possible solution. Be careful though, as in some cases it may not be the winning choice. In fact, graph databases provide integrated libraries that implement algorithms based on graph theory. These features allow for the computation of advanced statistics based on the graph topology itself. MongoDB, which was not born as a graph database, does not include these features. Therefore, if our application is going to exploit these algorithms, a graph database will best suit our needs.

The use of a document database, however, offers a greater modeling capability, which could be particularly useful for the implementation of some features of the application.

A final solution is the integration of two databases, a graph database and a document database in order to take full advantage of the potential of each technology. Although this approach is successful at first, a lot of attention must be paid. In fact, when different databases are used, data synchronization must always be taken into account. This implies that we will need to implement ad-hoc libraries to manage errors that can cause partial data writes. Moreover, the application will carry the burden of integrating the results of the queries issued to the various databases. These aspects will reduce performance and greatly complicate the application logic.

5.6 Storage engines in MongoDB

Which storage engine benefits from the pre-allocation model?

The storage engine is the component of each database responsible for data management. Starting with version 3.2, MongoDB uses WiredTiger, which provides several features, among which the following are present:

- concurrency control for writes at the document level
- MultiVersion Concurrency Control (MVCC)
- journaling and checkpoints
- compression libraries for both collections and indexes.

Until version 4.0, another storage engine called MMAPv1 was also available. Its peculiarity was that all documents were saved contiguously on disk. When a document became larger than the assigned space, MongoDB had to reposition it in a new disk location. This operation involved updating all the indexes and led to fragmentation of the disk space.

To avoid these reallocations, where possible, the pre-allocation model was used. In this way, the structure of the document was determined in advance and a maximum size was set for fields that could vary. As analyzed in Chapter 4 "Designing an information system for a medical center", with the advent of WiredTiger this model is no longer strictly necessary, but it can still be an excellent solution to simplify the representation of data and their management at the application level.

CHAPTER 6
EXERCISES ON MODELS

In this chapter you will find some questions and answers to verify and understand, through brief examples, how to apply the models discussed in the chapters of Section II "Case Studies".

6.1 The product-supplier model

Assuming you have two collections for products and suppliers respectively, which model allows you to minimize read operations to extract product information integrated with that of the supplier?

In order to create the relationship between a product and its supplier we need a supplier_id field for each document in the product collection, containing the identifier (for example the ObjectId) of the supplier that distributes it. In this way, we represent a one-to-many (*1-N*) relationship between the instances (documents) of the two collections.

With such a solution, whenever it is necessary to recover the information of the supplier of a product, two options are available.

The first is to ask the application to run a first query to retrieve the products of interest and save them in a special data structure in memory. Subsequently, the application will have to run a second query that filters the suppliers according to the *supplier_id* values of the products previously selected. The last step will consist in updating the data structure in memory, to associate the information of each supplier with the supplied products. This approach requires, therefore, two database reads, in addition to dedicated application logic, which can be costly in terms of performance.

A second possibility is the use of the aggregation pipeline. The pipeline will consist of at least 2 stages. The first stage will filter the products according to the required criteria, while the second stage will perform a JOIN between the products of interest and the suppliers of the products themselves, through the *$lookup* function. The result of this operation will produce a document with the same structure as the product document, with the addition of a vector (called for example supplier) containing the supplier documents that meet the JOIN condition.

Since according to the specifications each product is supplied by only one supplier, it is possible to convert the array into an embedded-document type field by simply applying the *$unwind* operator. This operator produces a document for each vector element, containing the original document with the value of the array field replaced by the i-th element. Figure 6.1 shows the pipeline used.

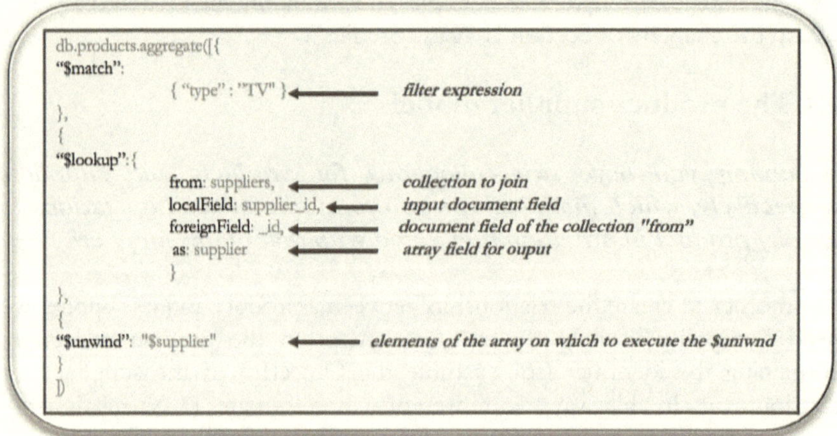

Figure 6.1 Aggregation pipeline to JOIN the products and suppliers collections.

The aggregation pipeline is certainly an excellent solution, as it allows us to generate the desired output with a single instruction. The disadvantage is that the execution time will be longer than accessing a single document. Also, if the collections are very large and the filtering criteria are not selective enough, CPU and memory resources may not be sufficient. In some cases, execution may even terminate with an error.

It is thus essential to understand whether all of the supplier's information is strictly required by the application. If only a subset of this information is relevant, the extended reference model would be the optimal solution. As seen in Chapter 2 "Designing an e-commerce website", this modeling pattern incorporates both the identifier of the referenced document (the supplier) and some of its information of interest, such as name and email address, in the referencing document (in the example, the product). In this way, we will need a simple query on the product collection to retrieve the minimum set of supplier information necessary for the application with a single operation. Should we need more supplier details, we can always apply the pipeline aggregation described above.

However, it should be kept in mind that the use of this model requires the application to appropriately propagate updates of the duplicate supplier fields.

6.2 How to manage the bestsellers of an e-commerce website

Our application manages an e-commerce site of books. Assuming we save, for each book, all the users who purchased it in an array-type field, how can we manage bestsellers selling millions of copies?

According to the specifications, each document in the Book collection contains an array, called *sales*, with all the identifiers (ObjectId) of the users. Assuming that many of these books sold a few hundred copies at most, we will need to deal appropriately with cases that have enjoyed a very high sales volume. A book is considered a bestseller when thousands of copies are sold. In such cases, the size of the document would grow too much to be managed in an optimal way.

To overcome this problem, the outlier model is applied. We need to add a Boolean field called *extra_sales*, with a default value equal to false, to each document in the *book* collection, and set, at the application level, a default threshold N for the maximum size of the *sales* array. When a book is purchased by more than N users, the application should set the *extra_sales* field to *true*. This will indicate that the application will need to perform an additional query to retrieve all users who have purchased the book. Obviously, another collection will be necessary (if not already present) that keeps track of all the purchases made, containing both user and book identifiers.

To make the model even more expressive, we can also apply the pre-aggregation model. Add an *n_sales* field that will contain the total number of users who have purchased the book. In case the calculation is too expensive, we can apply the approximation pattern. The calculation of the total number of sales will be updated routinely in the background at predefined time intervals. Indeed, the number of sales is a statistic that most likely does not need to be highly accurate or updated in real time.

However, the use of these models requires the implementation of dedicated application logic both to manage the controlled growth of the *sales* array and to update the sales statistics.

6.3 Management of product characteristics

Which modeling pattern is best suited to track all product features for a comparison site?

As discussed in Chapter 2 "Designing an e-commerce website", products may have only a few characteristics in common, even if they belong to the same product category. A model that keeps track of any product characteristics in a simple way is therefore fundamental.

A first model that can be applied is that of polymorphism. Mongo allows us to create documents belonging to the same collection with very different data structures. The disadvantage of this solution is that each document could have a very different structure from its peers, requiring an ad-hoc implementation for its management. The query logic would therefore become very complex, just like the one related to the visualization of the results.

To address this shortcoming, a widely used solution is the attribute model. A *specs* vector is created for all the relevant specifications, as shown in Figure 2.4. The structure of the sub-documents of this vector will be roughly always the same. Referring to the example in Figure 2.4, we will have the following fields:

- k: it will contain the name of the specification, useful also in the visualization phase
- v: it will save the value relative to the characteristic of the object
- u (optional): it will store the unit of measurement, if necessary

The application of the attribute model, associated with the polymorphism of the subdocuments, allows a simplified application logic for the execution of queries, an optimization of the creation of indexes and a simplification of the libraries for result visualization.

6.4 Best hotel reviews

To speed up access to the most relevant reviews of a hotel, which model can be applied?

First of all, it is necessary to consider the structure of the database. In this use case, we will need a collection for hotels and one for reviews. Each review will contain, in addition to a numerical and descriptive evaluation, the identifier of the hotel to which it refers. Figure 6.2 shows examples of the documents belonging to the two collections.

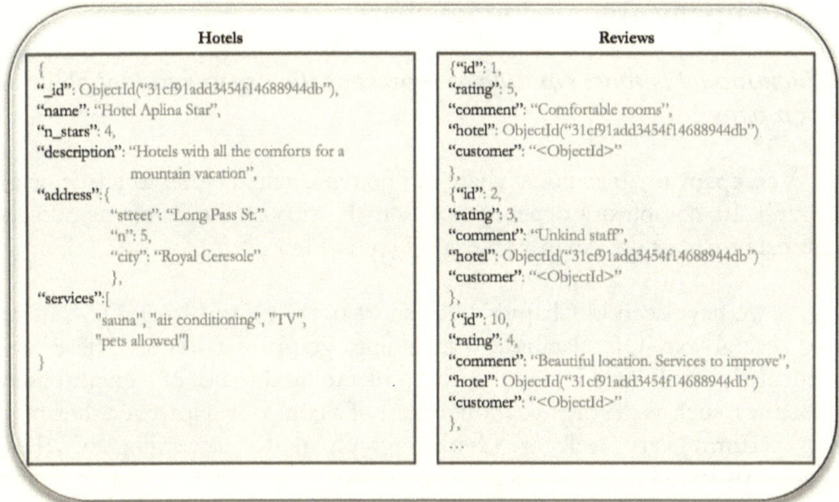

Figure 6.2 Examples of documents belonging to the hotels and reviews collections.

To access the reviews for a hotel, the application must necessarily query the *reviews* collection, filtered according to the hotel identifier and possibly additional criteria, to determine those of interest. The number of queries will be 2 – one to retrieve the hotel information and another to extract the most significant subset of reviews.

To reduce the number of queries, the subset model can be applied. Each hotel will have a vector-type field called *reviews*, which will track only the most significant ones. In this way, only one query will be performed to extract both hotel information and a predefined set of reviews. To access all the reviews, an additional query is needed. Since the retrieval of all reviews is an infrequent event and can be managed with result paging techniques, we will obtain a significant increase in the average performance.

However, dedicated application logic will be needed to update the reviews vector, according to certain criteria, each time a review is entered for a hotel. The criteria can depend on several factors. For example, we could select only the most recent top-k reviews, or those that have a descriptive field longer than a predefined threshold.

Updating the *reviews* vector of each hotel could be delegated to tasks that are performed in the background, at times when the system is not overloaded. It is not required that the most significant reviews should be updated in real time.

6.5 Company organizational chart

Which model is most suitable to represent the organizational chart of a company?

A company organizational chart can be represented either as a tree or as a graph. Its complexity depends both on the size of the company and its internal organization. An example is shown in Figure 6.3.

As we have seen in Chapter 1 "A short overview of MongoDB", there are several NoSQL databases, including graph databases. These are particularly well-suited for storing hierarchical and/or graph-based structures, such as the organizational chart of a company. However, they may not perform very well at filtering graph nodes according to their characteristics. They are typically more suitable to analyze the topology of the network or to navigate it.

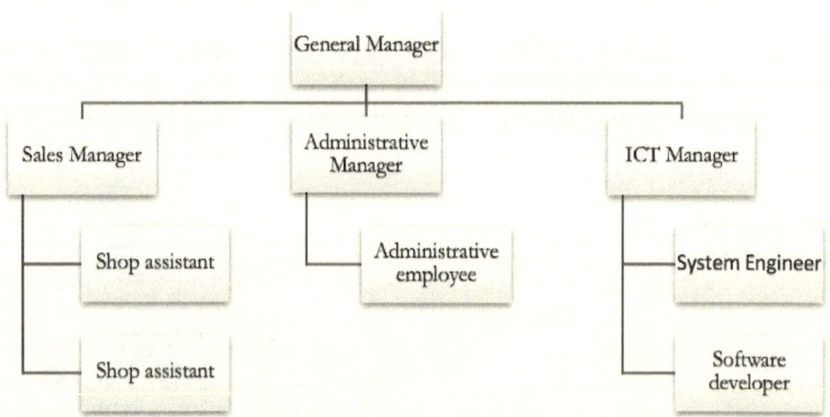

Figure 6.3 Tree representation of a company organizational chart.

Thanks to the aggregation pipeline, MongoDB allows the analyst to navigate documents even when they create a graph or a tree. We have seen that the *$graphLookup* function can be used for this purpose. Leveraging Mongo's potential to track and query even very heterogeneous documents, and the pipeline aggregation, we can design a database providing good performance, even in the presence of hierarchical structures. Unfortunately, Mongo does not embed any libraries implementing graph theory algorithms, which may come in handy for performing advanced analysis on the network topology. However, this aspect is usually not critical in the context of administrative applications.

The use of the aggregation pipeline requires significant resources to run, such that, in some cases, its execution may become very expensive. Queries may take several minutes if the graph is very large, or they may even not terminate due to lack of memory.

To overcome these problems, we can apply the tree model. Let's suppose for simplicity that the company organizational chart is a tree, where each staff member directly reports to only one superior. We add a new field, named *supervisor*, to each document in the *Employees* collection, which will contain the identifier of the staff member the employee reports to, or possibly a sub-document including her main information. To trace the entire chain of managers, up to the general manager, we add a hierarchy field that will save all of the employee's superiors, starting from the direct superior up to the general manager. An example document is shown in Figure 6.4.

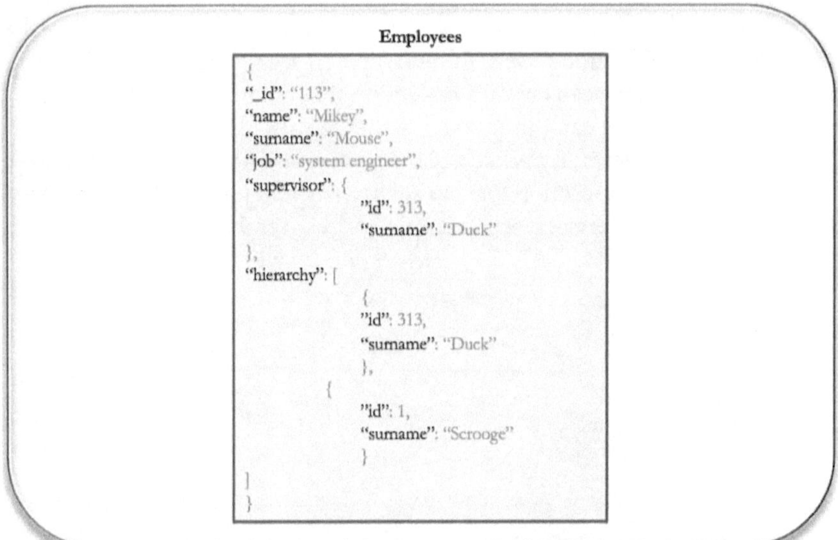

Figure 6.4 Example of a document related to an employee including the tree hierarchy of direct superiors.

In this way, we can get a quick overview of the command hierarchy without having to run an aggregation pipeline. As mentioned in Chapter 2 "Designing an e-commerce website" this model can be applied when there are no frequent changes in the hierarchy. A business organization chart falls into this scenario, as it is assumed that staff turnover does not occur frequently.

6.6 Integration of different business services

Assuming that a company acquires over time other companies operating in different industries, which modeling pattern allows to quickly integrate data from each new sector?

Each company that is acquired has many databases, each of which models the services offered, in different ways. Even the technologies they use can be very different from each other. If we wanted to integrate all the databases of the various services offered into a single relational database, the process could be long and particularly expensive. Moreover, it would be necessary to rewrite most of the applications to manage the heterogeneity of the various models.

Data warehouses are not a viable choice either, because they are designed to save aggregate measurements in order to speed up the generation of reports and statistics. In addition, ETL processes may take some time to extract all the data of interest, thus feeding the data warehouse with relatively old data.

To reduce the time and cost of merging different models, the polymorphic model can be used. For example, if we are integrating different telephony services, we can create a collection that contains the description of the active services for each user, even if they greatly differ in terms of their technical characteristics. By adding a *service_type* field to each document, we can implement the application logic in such a way that it can properly manage the various types of services. An example is shown in Figure 6.5.

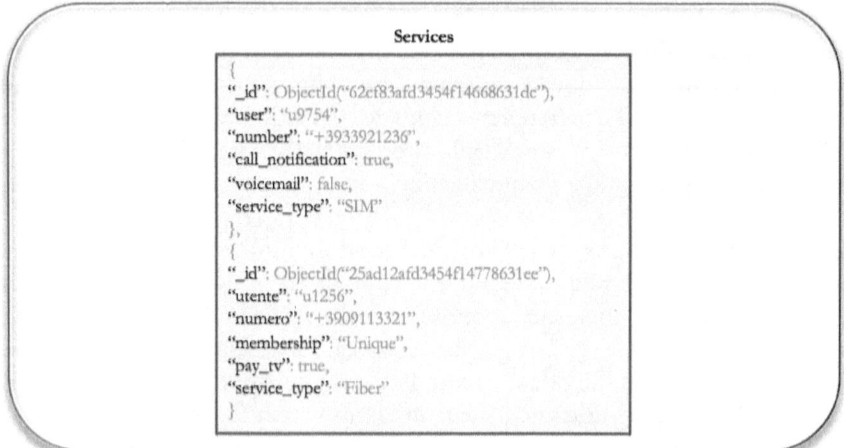

Figure 6.5 Example of telephone service documents from different providers.

6.7 Trace the logs of information systems

Which model can be applied for storing thousands of log lines coming from different information systems?

Nowadays, almost all computer systems produce textual output to keep track of occurring events. These texts are called logs and are usually saved to files. The rate at which this data is generated depends on the context, but it is in many cases high. The analysis of the logs is fundamental to identifying system anomalies and/or monitoring user activity.

Several commercial tools dedicated to the management of these data flows are available. Apache Kafka [8] is among the most used in the industrial field. Obviously, they represent dedicated systems that are placed side by side with other databases and software to respond to specific needs.

In case we want to integrate log management in a Mongo database, one possibility is the use of the bucket model in order to prevent the size of the database from growing exponentially. A collection, called *log*, will be used to save all the data coming from the various information systems that we want to monitor. Each document will contain a series of events recorded by a given platform in an interval of time. In this way it will be possible to easily extract all the documents related to log events for an information system of interest.

Considering that computer platforms can experience very different traffic volumes, also the logs of the events generated will be extremely variable, both in size and time frequency. Therefore, the definition of the bucket cannot be based on fixed time windows, since this may result in documents with very variable dimensions. Indeed, systems with a limited load and/or a small number of users will generate few events within a time window, while those accomplishing intensive work will produce large data flows, causing a significant increase in the document size.

To overcome the heterogeneity of the monitored information systems, the grouping strategy should be based on the number of events traced in each document. We can therefore suppose to keep track of 100 events in each document. If the *events* vector reaches a size of 100, the application will have to set an end date in the document and create a new one for the subsequent events. The resulting document structure is shown in Figure 6.6.

```
                                    Log

{
"_id": ": "<ObjectId>",
"id_is": 765,
"day": ISODate("2020-04-26T00:00:00.000Z"),
"start": ISODate("2020-04-26T18:05:00.000Z"),
"end": null,
"n_log": 68,
"events": [
        {
        "timestamp": ISODate("2020-04-26T18:05:00.000Z"),
        "message": "Duplicated entry (SQL)"
        },
        {
        "timestamp": ISODate("2020-04-26T18:05:50.000Z"),
        "message": "Click sign in button"
        },
        ...
]
}
```

Figure 6.6 Structure of a document containing log messages based on the bucket model.

6.8 City registry

To the aim of modeling the database of a city registry, which pattern can improve the performance of generating statistics on population distribution?

The city registry office has the task of tracking all citizens residing in its territory. This objective involves updating the database upon each new birth, death or transfer to another city/country. For small municipalities these events are not very frequent, while they occur daily for large metropolises.

We want to implement an information system, based on MongoDB, that can be used by any municipality, regardless of its size. The database will contain a collection for all the people who have been registered in the municipality. Using the *start_date* and *end_date* fields, the last period in which the person was resident in the municipality is indicated. If *end_date* takes on the *null* value, it means that the person is still resident.

In order to guarantee excellent performance, it is useful to consider the worst case during the planning phase, i.e. the one in which the updates occur very frequently, and the population is particularly numerous. Starting from this assumption, it is appropriate to understand which is the intended use of statistics relating to the resident population as foreseen by the municipal administration. Usually, these statistics are used to create periodic reports or to plan targeted investments in the area. Is it therefore necessary to have an exact and real-time estimate for these activities? Most likely, not. In fact, choices made by the municipal administration will not change drastically if the estimate of the population distribution is not exact to the level of a single unit. Hence, it is possible to apply the approximation model.

This model requires the application to perform statistical update tasks either at predefined intervals, or after a certain number of database writes.

A collection will be created, called *stats*, which will contain the statistics of interest. In this way, we will query only the documents in this collection to view the aggregated data, without having to perform the calculation on the *people* collection.

Applying the policy at regular intervals, for example, every week, we will get a limited and well-defined number of writes. This strategy is very simple to implement but has some limitations. In fact, if we define a time interval between runs of statistics updates that is too long, the *stats* collection data may become obsolete. Another disadvantage is the use of resources to calculate aggregate measurements even when there is no such need. Even if no updates have been made, we will still run the calculation process, which will use resources unnecessarily.

A different strategy is to track the number of updates made. If they exceed a certain threshold, then the statistics will be updated. At the application level, this requires a slightly more complex implementation, but avoids allocating resources if there are no significant updates. Care should be taken exercised, however, in defining the threshold that triggers the calculation process. If this threshold is too low, there is a risk of having a very frequent number of statistical updates that could overload the system.

Regardless of the chosen strategy, the approximation model will significantly reduce the number of writes and reads on the databases, as well as the resources employed by the system. By using documents from the *stats* collection, we can quickly generate reports, regardless of the size of the database.

6.9 Optimizing a time series database

To keep our database of measurements from different devices leaner, what strategies and models can we apply?

First, we need to analyze the problem of capturing measurements. As seen in Chapter 3 "Designing an energy consumption monitoring system", the appropriate model for optimizing the management of measurements generated by different devices is the bucket model.

In order to define the best strategy for the definition of the groups, we should analyze the characteristics of the devices and, in particular, the frequency of the measurements sent. If the devices are similar and apply a policy to submit their measurements that remains equal and constant over time, the grouping criterion can be based on the definition of fixed time intervals. Otherwise, we will group a predefined number of measurements for each device in each document.

To speed up the calculation of measurement statistics, we can apply the model of pre-aggregated values. We will add to each document the fields related to the statistics of interest, such as minimum, maximum and total. The average can be simply calculated as the total divided by the number of elements in the measurement array. The measurement array will only be used if we want to analyze the individual measurements in detail.

Regardless of the strategy adopted, we will obtain a database that is "lighter", i.e. take up less disk space, than a solution saving a new document for each individual measurement. Unfortunately, the accumulation of measurements over time will generate more and more documents, making our database very large.

Therefore, it is crucial to analyze whether the detail of the measurements is strictly necessary, even after a long period of time. If not, we can create a Time-To-Live (TTL) index for the collection of measurements on the *end_date* attribute. All documents whose value for this field is lower than a certain date, or time interval, will be automatically deleted. The size of the database will therefore not grow beyond a certain limit.

In order not to lose the statistics of documents that are too "old", and to speed up data retrieval, it is possible to define a routine at the application level. Using the pre-aggregated values model, the routine will calculate the statistics for all those documents that belong to a specific time interval. The result will be saved in a dedicated collection. Figure 6.7 shows the collection schema used for this type of example.

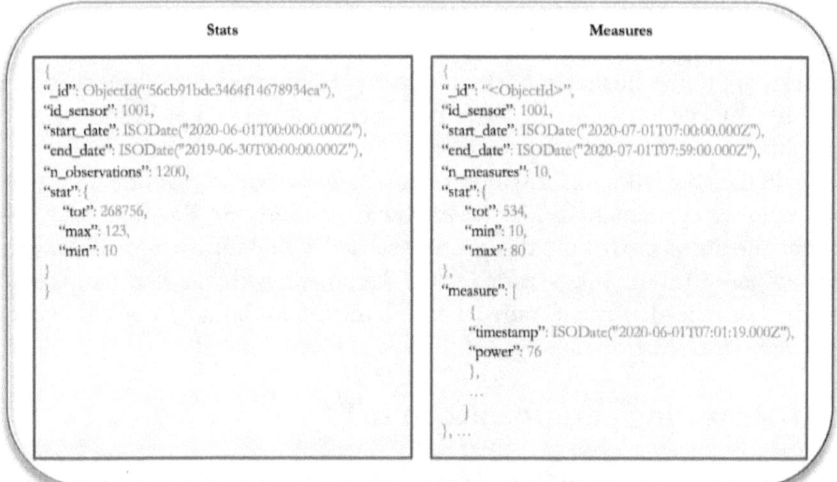

Figure 6.7 Collections used to store measurements from different devices. The structure of the measurement document is based on the bucket and pre-aggregated values models. Statistics documents are used to save aggregated data from historical periods.

6.10 Website traffic monitoring

Assuming you want to monitor the traffic of different websites, which aggregation strategy is most effective using the bucket model?

Many websites use tools to monitor user activity. The most used is undoubtedly Google Analytics. Through this tool, the owner of the site can analyze visits to its site by identifying both the means of acquisition (organic, social, direct), and some information on the types of users (geographical location, age, gender, etc.). Thanks to the use of this data, it is possible to define marketing strategies to improve the website presence on search engines and, consequently, the productivity of the site itself.

To create a similar tool, we can use Mongo in order to save all the data collected during navigation by users. To model the database correctly, we must consider the information related to website navigation as a flow of data that is not constant over time. Although the data collected will have a default structure regardless of the website being monitored, the strategy for sending it will depend on the number of visits received.

A very popular website can reach thousands of visits per minute, while other websites may have as few as some dozens of visits per day. For this reason, the density of the data collected can vary greatly.

Considering the navigation data as a flow that is not constant over time, we can apply the bucket model with an aggregation strategy, based on the number of events acquired. Each document will have a reference to the monitored website and a vector of sub-documents, called *events*, which will contain the navigation information received. We will an *n_events* field to track the number of elements in the *events* vector, and a *start_date* field that will match the timestamp of the first event recorded within the document. Finally, the *end_date* attribute will be added to the document, with the timestamp value of the last recorded event, only when the maximum limit of tracked events has been reached.

6.11 Measuring performance in IoT

To minimize the use of resources and database writes, what patterns can be applied to calculate performance scores in an IoT system?

Internet-of-Things (IoT) systems are based several devices connected over a network. Each device has the task of measuring certain properties that can range from environmental parameters (temperature, humidity, etc.) to the functional parameters of the devices themselves (power consumption, battery, etc.).

A centralized system is used to collect this information in order to provide an overview of the operation of the various devices and identify any anomalies until they are adjusted. For example, a system of environmental sensors can be used to regulate the operation of the heating system in a house in order to optimize energy consumption and reduce costs.

All information systems operating in this field use databases both to speed up the recovery of information and to provide a history of events that have occurred. As we have seen in Chapter 3 "Designing an energy consumption monitoring system", the best model to optimize the collection of measurements from various devices is the bucket model.

Regardless of the aggregation strategy used, which will be influenced by the characteristics of the devices, it is necessary to devise our model so that the calculations useful to determine the performance of our system are fast. For this reason, the bucket model is usually integrated with the pre-aggregated values model. This pattern defines some fields that hold aggregate measurements for each document.

When entering a new measurement, the system will also update the aggregated measurements of the document. Suppose that the documents for a device measure the temperature of the room in which it is placed. The measurement vector will contain the detail of each measurement taken in the time interval defined by the document. When a new measurement is sent from the device, it will be necessary to insert it into the measurements vector. With just one update instruction, we can update both the measurement vector and the total temperature measurement as well as the number of measurements in the document. Figure 6.8 shows the instruction.

```
db.measures.updateOne(
{
    "id_sensor": 1000,
    "start_date": ISODate("2020-08-01T09:00:00.000Z")
},
{
    $push: {
        "measures": {
            "timestamp": ISODate("2020-86-01T09:24:00.000Z"),
            "temp": 24
        }
    },
    $inc: {
        "n_measures": 1,
        "temp_tot": 24
    }
}
)
```

Figure 6.8 Update instruction to insert an item in the measurements vector and update the statistics.

In this way, the update operation is atomic. Moreover, we could calculate the performance indices in a very simple and effective way using the available pre-aggregated measurements.

6.12 Fast software release

To avoid service interruptions during a database schema update, which model is most convenient?

The rapid evolution of technologies and market demands require applications to evolve very quickly. The same applies to databases. Document databases such as MongoDB, which exploit polymorphism, can easily adapt to the evolution of the data structures that need to be stored.

Thanks to the polymorphism model, it is possible to save documents even with very different structures within the same collection. Unfortunately, the disadvantage of this model lies in the fact that the application needs to be constantly updated to manage documents with different data structures than those already present in the database.

The continuous stratification of application code changes can make it in most cases unmanageable. To overcome this criticality, we will usually opt for a re-modeling of the database and a rewriting of the code. This process, which can be time-consuming and expensive, ends with the production of the new application and the new database schema. Migration, however, is often very insidious and always requires an interruption of services.

Using the schema versioning model, service interruptions can be minimized. By inserting a field in each document, indicating the schema version used to save data within the document, we can create applications that use this information to operate correctly.

```
Contacts
{
"_id": "<ObjectId>",
"name": "Alessandro",
"surname": "Fiori",
"telephone": "+39-0123-1234",
"email":"alessandro.fiori@flowygo.com",

...

}
```

Figure 6.9 Example of a document to track the information of a contact in the address book.

Let us consider a web application for the management of an address book.

This application will initially save each contact with a very simple structure, shown in Figure 6.9.

Over time, we may notice that the fields that were initially designed are no longer sufficient and that we should use the attribute model to manage all contact modes for each phonebook entry. This involves rewriting the database, but also requires a substantial change in the structure of the documents. Using the schema versioning, we can update the application so that each time a contact is inserted or updated, the information is saved using the new schema (Figure 6.10). Conversely, when reading, the application will use different display templates according to the schema. Release these changes into production will not require a service interruption, since we can restart the web server (e.g. nginx) without any downtime.

Contacts

```
{
"_id": "<ObjectId>",
"name": "Alessandro",
"surname": "Fiori",
"contacts":[
                "telephone": "+39-0123-1234",
                "email": "+39-0123-5634,
],
"schema_version":2
},
{
"_id": "<ObjectId>",
"name": "Francesco",
"surname": "Rossi",
"telefphone": "+39-0123-5678",
"email":"francesco.rossi@email.it",
"schema_version":1
}
```

Figure 6.10 Documents that use schema versioning to track different data structures.

6.13 Theatre Information System

Assuming you have to model a seat reservation system for a theater, which modeling pattern can you use?

The reservation system of a theater requires a seat map. The main problem is that the arrangement of the seats depends on the size of the hall, the acoustics and the construction project. A notation from the famous battleship game is typically used to identify seats more easily. Each seat will be uniquely identified by a progressive number relative to the row it belongs to.

It is therefore possible to create a model that contains, for each show, the list of seats, and is able to tell us which ones have already been booked. An example is shown in Figure 6.11.

```
                              Shows

                {
                "_id": "<ObjectId>",
                "day": ISODate("2020-09-01T18:03:00.000Z"),
                "title": "The Imaginary Invalid",
                "seats": [
                                {"id": "A1", "reserved":false},
                                {"id": "A2", "reserved":true},
                                {"id": "B1", "reserved":true},
                                ...

                    ]
                }
```

Figure 6.11 Model for booking shows. The seats reported are only the existing ones.

The disadvantage of this model is that the application will have to calculate the real seating arrangement each time to provide a graphical representation of the room occupation. This calculation may slow down the system or require additional data structures, especially in cases where not all rows have the same number of seats.

Using the pre-allocation scheme, we can model the physical structure of the seats also at the database level. We need to create an initial empty structure for each show, to be filled later. The structure will be a two-dimensional array. Each cell of this array represents a seat with its related information.

For seats that do not exist, we can apply two distinct solutions: the subdocument of the two-dimensional array can have an *exists* field set to *false* or, alternatively, a *null* value can be inserted instead of the subdocument. In this way, it will be very easy to represent and identify the existing and occupied places. The document related to a show is depicted in Figure 6.12.

```
{
"_id": "<ObjectId>",
"day": ISODate("2020-09-01T18:03:00.000Z"),
"title": "The Imaginary Invalid",
"seats": [
    [{"id": "A1", "reserved": false, "exists": true}, {"id": "A2", "reserved": true, "exists": true}],
    [{"id": "B1", "reserved": true, "exists": true}, {"id": "B2", "reserved": false, "exists": false}],

    ...

  ]
}
```

Figure 6.12 Pre-allocated structure containing a matrix representation of the theater seats. Non-existing seats are marked with the Boolean field "exists".

6.14 Insurance policy management

Which application scenario can benefit from the document versioning model?

As discussed in Chapter 4 "Designing an information system for a medical center", the document versioning model is used to track the various changes a document undergoes over time. It is used in many highly regulated industries that require tracking all versions of a data set. Examples include financial, healthcare, legal and insurance.

The models seen in Chapter 4 "Designing an information system for a medical center", for example, can be very easily adapted to the insurance context. Policies, in fact, usually have a basic coverage that is personalised for each client with additional clauses and/or coverage. In addition to the current status of the policy, it is essential for the insurance company to have a view of historical changes in the client's policies. This makes it possible, for example, to set up appropriate advertising campaigns, create new insurance products or propose incentives to the most deserving clients.

As in the case of informed consent, the assets covered by each client's insurance policies do not undergo many variations over their lifetime. In addition, day-to-day queries are mainly carried out on the current version, while the history is used for periodic analysis.

The database will contain a document for each customer in the *insurances* collection storing all information about the policy, while the *insurance_reviews* collection will hold the documents for their previous versions. Also in this case, it is possible to create a collection containing the templates of the various policies, and make it available to the insurance company. Figure 6.13 shows some examples of documents belonging to the database collections.

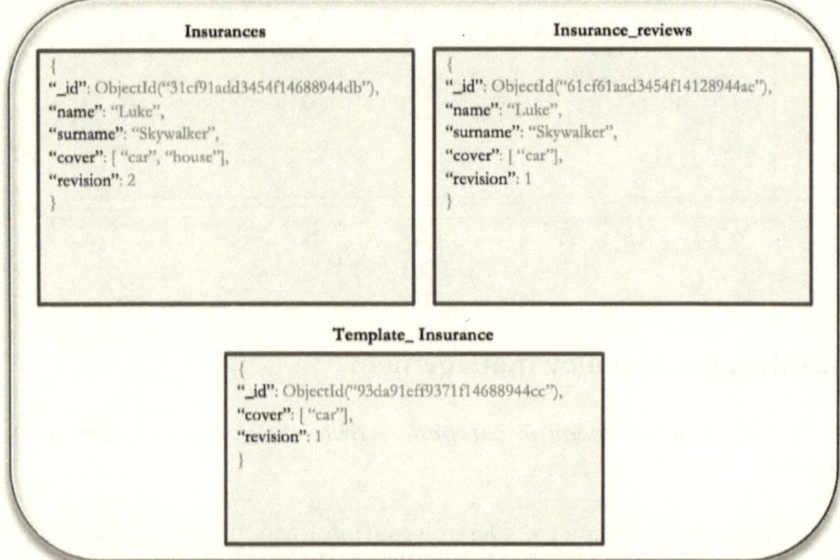

Figure 6.13 Collections for insurance policy management.

CONCLUSIONS

The case studies analyzed have made it possible to explore the most widely used modeling patterns and to better understand how to apply them. As we have seen, a good document schema design will have a significant impact on the performance of the application. The software is not necessarily responsible for any criticality in the applications accessing the database. Rather, it might be necessary to thoroughly investigate whether the model has been built appropriately in order to perform best in the application context of interest. This last consideration has always been valid since databases existed, but it is even more significant with NoSQL databases, where the database should adapt to the application and the data, and not vice versa.

This is one of the main reasons why programmers have been favoring NoSQL over relational databases in recent years. There are of course many other reasons. Some of them are as follows:

Reduction of database modeling time
> Since we don't have to define an a priori structure for our database, we can write an application that populates the database very quickly. Through the schema versioning model, for example, we can modify it just as quickly, without compromising the functionality of our application.

Easy code update
> Thanks to polymorphism, the database will easily adapt to changes in data structures. As a result, updates of the application code and its maintenance will also be much easier.

Reduced data manipulation

Unlike relational databases, document databases like Mongo can save data in a format equal, or very close, to the original data received by the application. Unlike with relational databases, there is often no need to create ETL (Extract, Transform, Load) processes to manipulate the received data and adapt them to the database structure. Today, many applications transmit their data using the JSON format, which is the format preferred by Mongo and his siblings.

Scalability

NoSQL, in general, was born to offer a product that is natively scalable. The typical Mongo production configuration includes a replica set with 3 nodes, which is also Mongo Atlas' default setup. Unlike in the relational case, the developer does not have to worry about configuring the database, thinking about how to distribute the data and how to optimize the workload. The NoSQL database will take care of most of these tasks, leaving room for modeling and application optimization.

Modeling patterns allow, therefore, not only for database structure optimization, but also for better, application data-oriented coding. The examples described here are just some of the many in which the analyzed patterns can be applied. As mentioned above, depending on the application, the use cases, the type and structure of the data to be managed, some of them will be more effective than others. The flexibility of Mongo and its document model is incredibly powerful, but care must be taken to exploit it properly. It is essential to always consider how to access data and in particular the ratio between writes and reads, the frequency of update for some fields and the structure of the most frequent queries.

The objective of this book is to provide the necessary tools to make the best choices during the design of a non-relational database – and in particular a document database. The fact remains that modeling is creativity, as there is no single solution to a problem. Possessing the right tools, however, is essential to achieving the best results!

Next steps

The use of modeling patterns is a first step to developing new generation applications and restructuring old programs and databases. What has been described in this book is a starting point for a grand tour of the data world.

Further insights into this text or other topics related to the web world can be found at https://flowygo.com.

Have a good journey!!!

BIBLIOGRAPHY

[1] D. Coupal and K. W. Alger, "Building with patterns," [Online]. Available: https://www.mongodb.com/blog/post/building-with-patterns-a-summary. [Accessed 15 June 2020].

[2] "Manuale MongoDB," [Online]. Available: https://docs.mongodb.com/manual/. [Accessed 01 September 2020].

[3] "Woocommerce," [Online]. Available: https://woocommerce.com/. [Accessed 01 September 2020].

[4] "Magento," [Online]. Available: https://magento.com/. [Accessed 01 September 2020].

[5] "Shopify," [Online]. Available: https://www.shopify.com/. [Accessed 01 September 2020].

[6] "Schema," [Online]. Available: https://schema.org/. [Accessed 01 September 2020].

[7] "Neo4j," [Online]. Available: https://neo4j.com/. [Accessed 01 September 2020].

[8] "Apache Kafka," [Online]. Available: https://kafka.apache.org/. [Accessed 01 September 2020].

ABOUT THE AUTHOR

Alessandro Fiori holds a PhD in Computer and Systems Engineering and is a developer of information systems for various scientific research realities. Adjunct Professor of Databases and Data Science at the Polytechnic of Turin, he has published more than 40 articles in international journals and has been publisher of some books dealing with scientific research topics on data mining.

He has followed several research projects for the development of information systems. Passionate about databases and open source, he develops his work using the latest technology. In particular, in the last years, he started to use MongoDB as reference database for the various projects. The experience gained with the use of this NoSQL database has led him to collect the material for the writing of this text as well as to create training courses for small-medium enterprises.

Over the last few years, he has collaborated in the development of several sites, including a cashback site to fund non-profit associations and a site for comparing digital photography products (https://camerarace.com/). The latter experience has brought him closer to the world of online business, developing site and blog development skills and increasing his knowledge of web applications development, SEO, search engine positioning techniques and results analysis.